AN IONA ANTHOLOGY

August 1992

Iona with Tom

- Thank the Lord That There are
Still Beautiful days to be Shared -

 W9-CUQ-492

AN IONA ANTHOLOGY

BY
F. MARIAN McNEILL

THE NEW IONA PRESS

First published 1947 by Eneas MacKay, Stirling.
Second edition 1952 by The Iona Community, Glasgow.
Reprint of second edition 1971 by The Albyn Press,
Edinburgh and London.
Third edition 1990. This is a new paperback edition
of the 1952 text, published by The New Iona Press Ltd,
Old Printing Press Building, Isle of Iona, Argyll.

© The Iona Community, 1990

ISBN 0 9516283 0 5

*The cover shows Iona Cathedral in the early 1930s,
photographed by Donald B. MacCulloch.*

Printed and bound in Great Britain
by Bell and Bain Limited, Glasgow.

TO
MY SISTER MARGARET

Peaceful scene at
Port Bàn, Iona,
photographed by
Donald B. MacCulloch,
about 1928

ACKNOWLEDGMENTS

The Editor and Publishers offer sincere thanks to the following authors and publishers who have given permission to quote copyright poems and prose extracts:—

Mr. Lewis Spence for *To The Islands*.

Mr. Noel Sharp for passages from *Iona; The Sin Eater and Other Legendary Moralities; The Three Marvels of Iona;* and *The Isle of Dreams* all by Fiona Macleod.

The late Rev. E. C. Trenholme for passages from *The Story of Iona*.

George Routledge & Co., Ltd., for extracts from Mr. Wentworth Huysshe's translation of Adamnan's *Life of St. Columba*.

Mr. Hugh MacDiarmid (C. M. Grieve) and B. T. Batsford, Ltd., for passages from *The Islands of Scotland*.

Rev. Dr. Kenneth Macleod for various poems.

Blackie & Son, Ltd., for an extract from *The Literature of the Celts* by Magnus Maclean.

Mr. Neil M. Gunn and Faber & Faber, Ltd., for passages from *Off in a Boat*.

Oliver & Boyd, Ltd., for poems from *Carmina Gadelica* edited by Alexander Carmichael.

The Most Reverend the Archbishop of St. Andrews and Edinburgh, for the *Collect for the Feast of St. Columba*, and Father Kenneth Cox for passing the translation.

The Cambridge University Press for the *Collect for the Feasts of SS. Kentigern, Patrick, Columba and Ninian* from *The Scottish Prayer Book*, 1929.

Miss Isobel Wylie Hutchison for four poems.

The Oxford University Press for an extract from *The Letters of John Keats* edited by M. Buxton Forman.

The Executors of the Matthay Estate and Boosey & Hawkes, Ltd., for a passage from *The Life of Tobias Matthay* by Jessie Henderson Matthay.

Jackson, Son & Co. (Booksellers), Ltd., for a passage from *Scottish Reminiscences* by Sir Archibald Geikie.

Mr. G. E. Troup for extracts from an address broadcast by him.

The Executors of the late Professor Macneile Dixon for two poems from *In Arcadia*.

Mrs. Bessie J. B. MacArthur and the Editor of *Chambers's Journal* for *Port na Churaich*, and Mrs. MacArthur and the Editor of the *Glasgow Herald* for *Iona*.

Mr. Robert Farren and Messrs. Sheed & Ward, Ltd., for three extracts from *The First Exile*.

Mr. Archie Lamont for a sonnet.

Miss Marion Lochhead for a poem.

Miss Agnes A. C. Blackie for a poem.

Miss Helen B. Cruickshank for two poems.

Miss I. F. Grant for a passage from *The Lordship of the Isles*.

Mr. Padraic Colum for his poem *Men on Islands*.

PREFACE

Florence Marian McNeill was born in 1885 in Orkney, where her father, Daniel McNeill, was a minister. After attending schools in Kirkwall and Glasgow, she graduated from Glasgow University. She was on the staff of the Scottish National Dictionary in Aberdeen for some years, becoming principal assistant by 1929. Scots language, culture and history were to be life-long interests, as was Scottish politics—while in her twenties she was Organiser of the Scottish Federation of Women Suffrage Societies and in later life was a Vice-President of the Scottish National Party.

F. Marian McNeill first visited Iona in 1917 and, finding no handbook concise yet comprehensive enough to suit her, resolved to write her own. The result, *Iona. A History of the Island*, was her first publication and appeared in 1920. She became a regular contributor to Scottish newspapers and magazines and her second foray into books came in 1929 with *The Scots Kitchen*. This soon gained its deserved reputation as a classic work on the traditional recipes and culinary history of Scotland. From 1957 to 1968 she brought out, in four volumes, *The Silver Bough*. In a scholarly yet lively way these document the folklore, customs and festivals of the whole country and have made an extremely important contribution to the collection and understanding of Scotland's traditions.

An Iona Anthology was first published in 1947. It is a richly varied selection of writings about Columba and Iona, reflecting the editor's own affection for the island and her interest in its history. Her choice includes several prayers and poems attributed to Columba plus some of the best-loved episodes from the Saint's life, as told by his biographer Adamnan. Other pieces range from E. C.

Trenholme's descriptive "View from Dun I" to Celtic hymns and blessings collected by folklorist Alexander Carmichael; from a factual account of the islanders' suffering after the 1846 potato famine to poems celebrating the peace and beauty of Iona. There are quotations by famous travellers to the island and tributes by figures from the world of Scots, Gaelic and English literature.

F. Marian McNeill died in 1973, two years after the last edition of her popular anthology appeared. The New Iona Press is pleased to publish this reprint, in recognition of all she has done to bring the history and traditions of Iona—and Scotland—to a wider audience. We hope that readers will continue to enjoy this collection for many years to come.

E. Mairi MacArthur
June 1990

INTRODUCTION

THERE are over five hundred islands in the Hebrides or Western Isles of Scotland. Many are famed in song and story, but it is one of the smallest that has achieved the widest and most splendid fame of all. It bears the lovely, evocative name of Iona.

Curiously the name Iona originates in the mistake of a medieval scribe in the copying of a manuscript. The original Pictish name is Iou, later Iou-a, which means (in Professor Watson's view) Yew-island. It was natural, he says, to connect the longest-lived of trees with health and long life, and Iona may well have been the seat of a yew-cultus. Other forms of Iou are Eo, Ea, Io, Ia. In modern Gaelic Iona is called I (pronounced ee), meaning *the* island; other spellings being Y, Hy, Hi, and Hii. It has two other Gaelic names as well: *Innis nan Druidhneach*, Isle of the Druids, and *Icolmkill*, the Island of Columba of the Cell or Church. The former gives substance to the tradition that before the coming of Columba Iona was a sacred island of the Druids; the latter commemorates the island's golden age.

How is it, it has been asked, that successive adorations come to be consecrated on the low, bare island of Iona, which from the dawn of history seems to wear a misty halo? Possibly its geology has something to do with it;

for Iona, like the Outer Hebrides, is formed of Archæan rock, and is immeasurably older than the adjoining islands —older, indeed, than the greater part of the earth's surface. But that is merely the present writer's speculation. There is, however, or was, archæological evidence to support the tradition of its having been a Druidical centre.

Druidism, which preceded Christianity in Scotland, lived amicably with it, side by side, for many generations, and still colours the newer religion in the West, was a form of sun-worship peculiar to the Celtic peoples. Adamnan, St. Columba's biographer, gives us many instances of the saint's encounters with the Pictish Druids.

The pre-Columban history of Iona is not history but legend. The cult of Druidism on the island has been imaginatively reconstructed by Fiona Macleod. To this period, too, belongs the legendary figure of St. Bride of the Isles—the lovely, tender-hearted herd-maiden who is transported by angels from Iona to Bethlehem on the eve of the Nativity to become aid-woman to Mary and foster-mother to the infant Jesus. This bride is, in fact, a purely imaginary figure who symbolises the transition from Druidism to Christianity. The original Bride was the fair young Celtic goddess of Spring, and St. Bride of the Isles, who links her with the seventh-century Irish saint, St. Bride of Kildare, is simply, in Sir James Frazer's words, " the pagan goddess in a threadbare Christian cloak."

The authentic history of Iona begins in 563, when Columba, accompanied by twelve companions, sailed thither from Derry in a coracle of wicker and hides. On the hill just west of Port-na-Curaich (the Cove of the Coracle), where he landed, is a small cairn called Carn Cul-Ri-Erin (the Cairn of the Back-to-Erin). Here, it is said, Columba scanned the southern horizon, and, satisfied

6

that Ireland was out of sight, buried the coracle on the beach and entered into possession.

Adamnan's *Life of St. Columba* is one of the treasures of history and is claimed as the most complete piece of such biography that Europe can boast of, not only at so early a period, but throughout the whole Middle Ages. The biographer (679-704) was the most famous Abbot of Iona after the Founder, and being born only twenty-seven years after the death of the Saint, had conversed with men who had been Columba's monks. The *Life* is deeply tinged with the credulous spirit of the age; but while rejecting, or, better, rationalising the miraculous elements in the narrative, we may regard the biographical details as authentic.

Columba was by no means the first Christian missionary to Scotland. That honour belongs to St. Ninian—a Briton from the shores of the Solway—of whom, indeed, Columba may be claimed as a spiritual descendant; for the Irish saint was trained first by Finian of Moville, who was himself trained at St. Ninian's great missionary centre, Candida Casa (Whithorn) in Galloway, and later by St. Finian of Clonaid, whose own teachers, St. Eany of Aranmore and St. David of Llancarvan, had also been educated there. But the Pictish Church established by St. Ninian covered only the south and east of Scotland, and Columba's task was to complete and consolidate the work of his great predecessor.

The personality and achievement of Columba were so remarkable that he early became a legendary figure. Like all saints, he was not devoid of human failings, and there were some turbulent episodes in his youth. He was of princely blood, and combined statesmanship with saintliness and great missionary zeal. In addition, he was a scholar

7

and gifted bard. By some modern critics he has been accused of being the political agent of the Irish kings of Dalriada (Argyll and the Isles). But even if such human weakness be admitted, it does not detract from the essential greatness of the saint's character. Padraic Colum sums up Columba as " the Gael of all time, impetuous, generous, winning; the champion of the oppressed in an age of barbarism, the holder of the Christian ideal, the creator of a small piece of civilization in Europe's dark age."

A new chapter in the island's history began in 1203, when, following on the Latinization of the Scottish Church by Margaret, Queen and Saint, a Benedictine monastery was established there by Reginald, Lord of the Isles. A nunnery followed, nuns of the Augustinian order succeeding the original Benedictines. This occupation of the island, which lasted up to the Reformation, proved uneventful, but is commemorated in the buildings now in process of restoration by the Iona Community.

Iona itself, to the casual eye, is little to look at. Yet it is beloved of artists—and of artists of distinction—who are drawn thither by its richness of colouring and its unique atmosphere. Unique? Almost, but not quite. Some years ago, the present writer, looking out, for the first time, from a window in the Scottish Mission Hospital in Tiberias across the Sea of Galilee to the bare, yet strangely appealing landscape beyond, became conscious that this atmosphere of austere beauty and deep peace was curiously familiar, and suddenly the name *Iona* leapt to her mind. A long summer in Iona, and an Easter in Galilee—these remain two of her most cherished memories.

F. MARIAN McNEILL

EDINBURGH.

8

CONTENTS

11

12

APPROACH TO IONA

TO THE ISLANDS

I will away to the Kyles
And the rain-showered Isles,
Mosses of the sea;
And on far elphin strands
And wide wind-wandered sands
I shall be free.

And in vast evenings straying
Shall watch the floods delaying
On the amber beach;
One with the winds and waves,
Rapt in the quiet that saves
All thought—all speech.

Lewis Spence

APPROACH TO IONA

Let us approach that sacred isle with more than common reverence: there, where now it lies in the midst of rolling billows, and listening but to sea-birds' cries, from age to age in the morning of early history, night and day it heard the sweet songs of God—the Psalms of David, the Church's hymns, and that never-ceasing anthem, " Thou art the King of Glory, O Christ."

Bishop Ewing: Iona

13

THE LAMP THAT LIGHTED PAGAN EUROPE

A few places in the world are to be held holy, because of the love which consecrates them, and the faith which enshrines them. Their names are themselves talismans of spiritual beauty. Of these is Iona.

. . . It is but a small isle, fashioned of a little sand, a few grasses salt with the spray of an ever-restless wave, a few rocks that wade in heather, and upon whose brows the sea-wind weaves the yellow lichen. But since the remotest days, sacrosanct men have bowed here in worship. In this little island a lamp was lit whose flame lighted pagan Europe, from the Saxon in his fens, to the swarthy folk who came by Greek waters to trade in the Orient. Here Learning and Faith had their tranquil home when the shadow of the sword lay upon all lands from Syracuse, by the Tyrrhene Sea, to the rainy isles of the Orc. From age to age, lowly hearts have never ceased to bring their burthen here. Iona herself has given us for remembrance a fount of youth more wonderful than that which lies under her own boulders of Dun-I. And here Hope waits. To tell the story of Iona, is to go back to God, and to end in God.

Fiona Macleod: Iona

BEHOLD IONA!

A BENEDICTION ATTRIBUTED TO COLUMBA

It was on the eve of Pentecost that those on the coracle sighted Iona. Columba improvised a chant on sight of the island, and the brethren repeated it as they sailed into the little haven.

Behold Iona!
A blessing on each eye that seeth it!
He who does a good for others
Here, will find his own redoubled
· Many-fold!

THE SETTING

ICOLUMKILL

Insula Pictorum quaedam monstratur in oris,
Fluctivago suspensa salo, cognominis Eo
Qua sanctus domini requiescit carne Columba.

Far on the Pictish coast is seen a sea-girded islet,
Floating amidst the billows: Eo the name that it beareth.
There the saint of the Lord, Columba, rests in the body.

Walafrid Strabo (ninth-century German monk).

THE LORD OF THE ISLES SAILS BY

Merrily, merrily goes the bark,
   Before the gale she bounds;
So darts the dolphin from the shark,
   Or the deer before the hounds.
They left Loch-Tua on their lee,
And they waken'd the men of wild Tiree
   And the Chief of the sandy Coll;
They paus'd not at Columba's isle,
Though peal'd the bells from the holy pile
   With long and measured toll;
No time for matin or for mass,
And the sounds of the holy summons pass
   Away in the billows roll.
Lochbuie's fierce and warlike lord
Their signal saw, and grasp'd his sword,
And verdant Ilay call'd her host,
And the clans of Jura's rugged coast
   Lord Ronald's call obey,

15

And Scarba's isle, whose tortured shore
Still rings to Corrievrekan's roar,
And lonely Colonsay;
—Scenes sung by him who sings no more!
His bright and brief career is o'er.
Sir Walter Scott: The Lord of the Isles, Canto IV.*

THE VIEW FROM DUN-I

Iona's geographical position . . . can be effectively realised on the spot by a survey of the wide and splendid view from the northern hill of the island. It lies in the midst of the Hebrides, or Western Isles of Scotland, and these varied islands, far and near, great and small, with their vast enchanting setting of ocean and sky, compose the whole of the prospect. A quarter of the circle is an unbroken sweep of water, beyond whose horizon Ireland is distant seventy miles, and Labrador two thousand. Of the islands which form most of the rest of the ring, all that were inhabited have known the monks of Iona, for this was their home mission field. To begin with Tiree, the long low island whose higher points appear at intervals above the waves twenty miles north-west. Here Iona had more than one monastery. . . . It is sometimes possible to discern a speck on the horizon more than twice as far out as Tiree. This is Barra Head, the southernmost islet of the long outer fringe of the Hebrides, a rock . . . with a lighthouse. When the dusk of evening settles on the ocean, Skerryvore revolving light flashes out, ten miles south of Tiree, where murderous rocks lie.

More to the north of Iona are the bare and rocky Treshnish Isles, and Coll's broken outline in the distance. Beyond the Treshnishes, forty miles north of Iona, rises the mountain island of Rum, where an Iona monk lived as a hermit in the seventh century. St. Donnan's Isle of Eigg is near. One summit in Rum stands out as a sharp peak,

* " I believe I shall make another adventure . . . upon a subject of Scottish history; I have called my work *The Lord of the Isles.* The greater part has been long written, but I am stupid at drawing real scenery, and waited until I should have a good opportunity to visit, or rather re-visit, the Hebrides."—W. S.

to the right of which the Cuillin hills in Skye are visible on a clear day. The Cuillins, sixty miles away, and reaching 3,230 feet in height, are the most distant and the loftiest mountains in sight.

. . . Mull is the large mountainous island between Iona and the mainland of Argyllshire, and its varied coast and more distant hills where the red deer roam fill most of the eastward view. The isles of Gometra and Ulva lie against the projecting coast of Mull above Iona, and in front of Gometra, Staffa's basalt cliff-face rises from the sea. Following down the Mull coast, a steep break in the hill-line marks where an arm of the sea runs into Mull, almost cutting it in two. This inlet is called Loch nan Ceall (Loch of the Churches), from the number of ancient churches that stood on its shores. The remains of one are in Inchkenneth, a small island seen from Iona in the mouth of the loch. . . . Sir Allan Maclean entertained Dr. Johnson and Boswell at his house in Inchkenneth in 1773, and brought them over to visit Iona.

The centre of the view of Mull is Ben More's cloudy summit. . . . The south of Mull is projected westward in a long tongue of land called the Ross, off the end of which lies Iona, separated by a Sound a mile in width. The granite rocks off the end of the Ross . . . in the foreground of the spectator's view . . . are very striking when silhouetted in black between the pallid sea and sky of early dawn, or when they glow rosy red in the warm light of the setting sun.

To the south-east the three rounded mountains rising side by side above the low line of the Ross are the Paps of Jura, thirty miles away. Islay is next to Jura, and Colonsay in front. The Ross itself ends with Earraid Isle, on which is seen the lighthouse station for Dubh Iartach and Skerry-vore Lights, and off Earraid a high outlying rock islet, Eilean nam Muc, stands sentinel over the southern entrance to the Sound, with the Torran Rocks lying beyond. Dubh Iarteach is a lighthouse perched on a solitary rock twelve miles south-south-west of Iona, and from it to Tiree nothing breaks the sweep of the sea-line.

E. C. Trenholme: The Story of Iona

17

AN ARCHÆAN ROCK

Iona itself is enormously older than these adjoining islands, and than the highest mountains and most of the dry land of the globe. . . . The beginning of Iona is almost part of the beginning of the earth itself. When our planet, from a flaming mass of combustion like the sun, shrivelled into a globe with a solid crust, and the first oceans condensed in the hollows of its hot surface—then it was that the Archæan rocks of which Iona and the Outer Hebrides consist were formed on the sea-bottom. They contain no fossils; for, so far as is known, no living creature as yet existed in the desolate waste of waters or on the primeval land.

E. C. Trenholme: The Story of Iona

MULL AND THE ISLES

And not only on the Machair and the Camus of Iona,
Portawherry, and Dun-I, upon the slopes of corn and clover,
    wandered Colm and his concourse; but they shot from
    off the shingles,
Off the creeks, and the sea-beaches, off the strands with the
    shell-tinkle,
To waves with white-stone paving, to waves like lilac tinted,
To waves like green stalks tossing blossoms of the white
    bog-myrtle;
And with oars and helm and canvas bested breeze and reef
    and current,
Coming swiftly to Colonsay, to Oronsay, and to Staffa,
Bringing ministry of sacrament, and God's word, like a
    torrent
To their kinsmen of the islands and their children, like a
    ladder.

Robert Farren: The First Exile

ST. COLUMBA

THE VISION OF ETHNE
THE MOTHER OF ST. COLUMBA

On a certain night, between the conception and the birth of the venerable man, the Angel of the Lord appeared to his mother in sleep, and, standing by her, brought her a certain mantle of marvellous beauty, in which lovely colours of all flowers were depicted; and, after a brief interval, he asked for it back, and took it from her hands, and raising and spreading it out sent it forth into the empty air. She, however, saddened by its being taken away, thus speaks to that man of venerable aspect: "Why does thou thus quickly take away from me this lovely mantle?" He immediately replies: "For the reason that this mantle belongs to one of such grandeur and honourable station that thou canst keep it no longer by thee." And, these words said, the woman saw the afore-mentioned mantle gradually receding from her in its flight, and increasing in size so as to exceed the width of the plains, and to overtop the mountains and forests, and then she heard this following voice: "Be not sorrowful, woman, for to the man to whom thou art joined by the marriage contract thou shalt bring forth a son so illustrious that, like one of the prophets of God, he will be numbered among them, and is predestined by God to be the leader of innumerable souls to the Heavenly Country." And while she hears this voice the woman awakes.

Adamnan: Life of St. Columba

19

COLUMBA'S FAREWELL TO IRELAND

In an ancient Irish poem which is in the form of a song of farewell, Columba thus describes his departure from his native land:—

How rapid the speed of my coracle,
And its stern turned upon Derry:
I grieve at my errand o'er the noble sea,
Travelling to Alba of the ravens,
My foot in my sweet little coracle,
My heart still bleeding.
Weak is the man that cannot lead;
Totally blind are all the ignorant.
There is a grey eye
That looks back upon Erin;
It shall not see during life
The men of Erin, nor their wives.
My vision o'er the brine I stretch
From the ample oaken planks;
Large is the tear of my soft grey eye
When I look back upon Erin.

COLUMBA REACHES IONA

" Kinsmen in Christ the Redeemer, God keep, God shield
   ye.
Now is the end of seeking our stall of exile;

.   .   .   .

Christ brought us here, kinsmen, is by us, waiting;
His Spirit this eve of Whitsun makes us apostles
Rousing our priesthood in us, speaking within us,
That we may speak Him unto a heathen people."

Kneeling on the new-seen earth they said " Benedicite——":
Children in a furnace of fervour for the harvest of the Gospel.

Robert Farren: The First Exile

IONA

Among the Irish manuscripts in the Burgundian Library of Brussels is an ancient Celtic poem bearing the title " Columcille fecit." This poem, says Dr. Skene, so remarkably describes the view from Carn-cul-ri-Erin, overlooking the Port-na-Curraich, and the emotions it was calculated to excite in one of Columba's temperament that it is hardly possible to avoid the conclusion that it contains the genuine expression of his feelings.

Delightful would it be to me to be in Uchd Ailiun
    On the pinnacle of a rock,
That I might often see
    The face of the ocean;
That I might see its heaving waves
    Over the wide ocean,
When they chant music to their Father
    Over the world's course;
That I might see its level sparkling strand,
    It would be no cause of sorrow;
That I might hear the song of the wonderful birds,
    Source of happiness;
That I might hear the thunder of the crowding waves
    Upon the rocks;
That I might hear the roar by the side of the church
    of the surrounding sea;
That I might see its noble flocks
    Over the watery ocean;
That I might see the sea monsters,
    The greatest of all wonders;
That I might see its ebb and flood
    In their career;
That my mystical name might be, I say,
    Cul-ri-Erin;
That contrition might come upon my heart
    Upon looking at her;
That I might bewail my evils all,
    Though it were difficult to compute them;
That I might bless the Lord
    Who conserves all,
Heaven with its countless bright orders,
    Land, strand, and flood;
That I might search the books all
    That would be good for any soul;

At times kneeling to Beloved Heaven;
At times at psalm-singing;
At times contemplating the King of Heaven,
Holy the Chief;
At times at work without compulsion;
This would be delightful.
At times plucking *duilisc* from the rocks;
At times fishing;
At times giving food to the poor;
At times in a *carcair* (solitary cell).
The best advice in the presence of God
To me has been vouchsafed.
The King whose servant I am will not let
Anything deceive me.

Translation by *Professor Eugene O'Curry*

COLUMBA REPUDIATES DRUIDISM

There is no *Sreod** that can tell our fate,
Nor bird upon the branch,
Nor trunk of gnarled oak . . .
Better is He in whom we trust
The King who has made us all,
Who will not leave me to-night without refuge.
I adore not the voice of birds,
Nor chance, nor the love of son or wife,
My Druid is Christ, the Son of God.

From The Song of Trust
(*an Old Irish Poem
attributed to Columba*)

THE VOICE OF ST. COLUMBA

The sound of the Voice of Columba,
Great its sweetness above all clerics:
To the end of fifteen hundred paces,
Though great the distance, it was distinctly heard.

From the Old Irish *Life*

* *Sreod*—An unknown Druidical term, probably meaning some
pagan superstition or rite.

COLUMBA VISITS BRUDE, KING OF THE PICTS, AT INVERNESS

At the time when the Saint was weary from his first journey to King Brude, it so happened that the king, elated by royal pride in his fortress, acting haughtily, did not open the gates at the blessed man's first arrival. And when the man of God knew this, he came with his companions to the wickets of the portals, and first traced on them the Sign of the Lord's Cross, and then knocking, he lays his hand against the doors, and immediately the bolts are violently shot back, the doors open in all haste of their own accord, and being thus opened the Saint thereupon enters with his companions. Upon this being known, the king, with his council, is greatly affrighted, and issues forth from his house to meet the blessed man with all reverence, and addresses him gently with conciliatory words. And from that day forth this ruler honoured the holy and venerable man with very great honour all the remaining days of his life; as was proper.

Adamnan: Life of St. Columba

COLUMBA AND THE DRUID

(At the court of King Brude, Columba makes the acquaintance of Briochan, his Chief Druid)

After the above-mentioned events, Broichan, speaking one day to the holy man, says: " Tell me, Columba, at what time dost thou propose to sail forth? " " On the third day," says the Saint, " God willing and life remaining, we propose to begin our voyage," " Thou wilt not be able to do so," says Broichan in reply, " for I can make the wind contrary for thee, and bring dark clouds upon thee." The Saint says, " The omnipotence of God rules over all things, in whose name all our movements, He Himself governing them, are directed." What more need be said? On the same day as he had purposed in his heart, the Saint came to the long lake of the River Ness, a great crowd following. But the Druids then began to rejoice when they saw a great darkness coming over, and a contrary wind with a tempest. Nor should it be wondered at that these things can be done by the art of demons, God permitting it, so that even winds and waters are roused to fury.

. . . Our Columba, therefore, seeing the furious elements stirred up against him, calls upon Christ the Lord, and entering the boat while the sailors are hesitating, he, with all the more confidence, orders the sail to be rigged against the wind. Which being done, the whole crowd looking on meanwhile, the boat is borne along against the contrary winds with amazing velocity. And after no great interval, the adverse winds veer round to the advantage of the voyage, amid the astonishment of all. And thus, throughout that whole day, the blessed man's boat was driven along by gentle favouring breezes, and reached the desired haven.*

Adamnan: Life of St. Columba

THE SEA-FARING MONKS

In these frail skiffs Columba and his monks ploughed the dangerous and stormy sea which dashes on the coasts of Scotland and Ireland, and penetrated boldly into the numberless gulfs and straits of the sombre Hebridean archipelago.

Montalembert: The Monks of the West

Wondrous the warriors who abode in Hi,
Thrice fifty in the monastic rule,
With their boats along the main sea,
Three score men a-rowing.

Old Irish Verse

COLUMBA AND THE LOCH NESS MONSTER

At another time also, when the blessed man was sojourning for some days in the province of the Picts, he was obliged to cross the River Ness†; and when he had come to the bank, he sees some of the inhabitants burying an unfortunate fellow, whom, as those who were burying

* The south-western end of the loch, where now stands St. Benedict's Abbey, Fort Augustus.

† The Ness, which flows out of Loch Ness into the Moray Firth. Inverness lies at its estuary.

him related, a little while before, some aquatic monster seized and savagely bit while he was swimming, and whose hapless body some men, coming up though too late in a boat, rescued by means of hooks which they threw out. The blessed man, however, hearing these things, orders one of his companions to swim out and bring him from over the water a coble that was beached on the other bank. And hearing and obeying the command of the holy and illustrious man, Lugne Mocumin without delay takes off his clothes, except his tunic, and casts himself into the water. But the monster, which was lying in the river bed, and whose appetite was rather whetted for more prey than sated with what it had already had, perceiving the surface of the water disturbed by the swimmer, suddenly comes up and moves towards the man as he swam in mid-stream, and with a great roar rushes on him with open mouth, while all who were there, barbarians as well as Brethren, were greatly terror-struck. The blessed man seeing it, after making the Salutary Sign of the Cross in the empty air with his holy hand upraised, and invoking the Name of God, commanded the ferocious monster, saying: " Go thou no further, nor touch the man; go back at once." Then, on hearing the word of the Saint, the monster was terrified, and fled away again more quickly than if it had been dragged off by ropes, though it had approached Lugne as he swam so closely, that between man and monster there was no more than the length of one punt pole. Then the Brethren greatly marvelling, seeing the monster had gone back, and that their comrade Lugne had returned to them in the boat, untouched and unharmed, glorified God in the blessed man. And even the barbarous heathens who were there present, constrained by the greatness of the miracle which they themselves had seen, magnified the God of the Christians.

Adamnan: Life of St. Columba

COLUMBA AND THE CRANE

At another time, when the Saint was living in the isle of Iona, calling one of the Brethren to him, he thus addresses him: " On the third day from this now dawning, thou must keep a look out in the western part of this isle, sitting on the sea-shore, for from the northern region of Ireland, a certain guest, a crane, driven by the winds through long, circling aerial flights, will arrive very weary and fatigued after the ninth hour of the day; and its strength almost exhausted, it will fall and lie before thee on the shore, and thou will take care to lift it up kindly and carry it to a neighbouring house, and there will hospitably harbour it and attend to it for three days and three nights, and carefully feed it; at the end of the three days, refreshed, and unwilling to sojourn longer with us, it will return with fully regained strength to the sweet region of Ireland, whence it originally came. And I thus earnestly commend it to thee for that it came from the place of our own fatherland."

The Brother obeys, and on the third day after the ninth hour, as commanded, he awaits the coming of the expected guest; and, when it comes, he raises it from the shore where it fell; carries it, weak as it was, to the hospice; feeds it in its hunger. And to him, on his return to the monastery in the evening, the Saint, not by way of enquiry but of statement, says: " God bless thee, my son, because thou hast well attended our stranger guest; and it will not tarry long in exile, but after three days will return to its country." And, just as the Saint predicted, the event also proved. For having been harboured for three days, raising itself on high by flight from the ground in presence of its ministering host, and considering for a little while its course in the air, it returned across the ocean to Ireland in a straight line of flight, on a calm day.

Adamnan: Life of St. Columba

A VISITATION OF ANGELS

Angels' Hill (in Gaelic, Cnoc an Aingeal, but better known locally as Sithean Mor, the great fairy-mound) is a round knoll of sand covered with green sward on the left of the road which leads to the Machair, on the west side of the island.

This is the traditional site of Columba's tryst with the angels. The prying Brother who witnessed the scene probably stood on the adjacent mound, Cnoc Odhrain, beside the croft of that name.

One day the holy man, then living in Iona, assembled the brethren together and charged them with great earnestness, saying to them: " To-day I wish to go alone to the western plain of our island; therefore let none of you follow me." And they complying, he goes forth alone as he wished. But a certain Brother, a cunning and prying man, going by another way, secretly posts himself on the top of a certain hillock which overlooks the same plain, desiring to find out the cause of the blessed man's going out alone. And when the same spy from the top of the hillock beheld him standing on a certain mound on that plain, and praying with hands spread out to heaven, and raising his eyes heavenwards, wonderful to say, behold! suddenly a marvellous thing appeared . . . For Holy Angels, citizens of the Heavenly Country, clad in white garments, flying to him with wonderful swiftness, began to stand around the holy man as he prayed, and after some conversation with the blessed man, that celestial band, as if perceiving that it was being spied upon, sped quickly back to the heights of the heavens. And the blessed man himself, having returned to the monastery after the angelic conference, and the Brethren being again assembled, he inquires with no little chiding which of them is guilty of disobedience. And they then protesting they did not know, he who was conscious of his inexcusable transgression, no longer able to hide his fault, suppliantly begs pardon in the midst of the choir of the Brethren in the Saint's presence. And the Saint leading him aside charges him, as he kneels before him, under heavy threats, that to no man must he reveal anything, even the least particle of the secret of that angelic vision, during the days of the same blessed man. But after the departure of the holy man from the body, he relates the apparition of the Heavenly host to the Brethren with solemn attestation.

Adamnan: Life of St. Columba

27

OF A CERTAIN SPIRITUAL CONSOLATION SENT BY THE HOLY MAN TO THE MONKS ON THEIR WAY BACK, WEARY FROM TOIL

Among these wonderful manifestations of prophetic spirit it does not seem out of place to commemorate also in our little record, a certain spiritual consolation which the monks of St. Columba felt on one occasion from his spirit meeting them by the way. For once, as the Brethren after harvest work, returning to the monastery in the evening, and arriving at that place which is called in Scotic (Irish) Cuuleilne, which place is said to be midway between the western plain of the island of Iona and our monastery,* they seemed each one to feel within himself something wonderful and unusual, which, however, they dared not speak of the one to the other. And so for some days, in the same place, and at the same evening hour, they perceived it. But in those days St. Baithene† was the superintendent of labours among them, and one day he spoke thus to them, saying: " Now, Brothers, if ye unexpectedly experience anything unusual and wonderful in this place, half-way between the harvest field and the monastery, ye ought to declare it, each one of you."

Then one of them, a senior, says: " According to thy order I will tell thee what has been shown to me in this place; for, in these days past, and even now, I perceive some fragrance of a marvellous odour, as if that of all flowers collected into one; and also a certain burning as of fire, not painful, but as it were soothing; and, besides, a certain unaccustomed and incomparable joy spread abroad in my heart, which of a sudden consoles me in a wonderful way,

---

* Half-way between the *Campulum*, the Machar, or plain, of the island of Iona and the monastery is a spot called Bol-lethne, which may be a corruption of the original name. From the narrative it would seem that it was here that the most laborious part of the way began, and at Bol-lethne there is an ascent, and the path becomes rugged."—*Wentworth Huyshe:* Note to Adamnan's Life.

† " He was one of the original companions of St. Columba, and was head of a monastic settlement in Tiree. In the narrative he was holding the office of *dispensator operum* in Iona. He became Abbot of Iona after St. Columba's death."—*Ibid.*

and so greatly gladdens me that I can remember sadness no more, labour no more. Aye! and the load, albeit heavy, which I am carrying on my back from this place until we come to the monastery, is so much lightened, how I know not, that I do not feel that I am bearing any burden." What more shall I say? So all the harvest workers one by one declare, each one for himself, that they had felt exactly as this one of them had first spoken, and one and all together on bended knee besought St. Baithene that he would let them know, ignorant as they were, the cause and origin of that wondrous consolation which he himself felt just as the rest perceived it. To whom, thereupon, he gave this answer saying, " Ye know that our senior, Columba, mindful of our toil, thinks anxiously about us, and grieves that we come to him so late; and by reason that he comes not in body to meet us, his spirit meets our steps, and that it is which so much consoles and makes us glad." And hearing these words, still kneeling, with great joy and with hands spread out to heaven, they venerate Christ in the holy and blessed man.   *Adamnan:* Life of St. Columba

PRAYER FOR THE KING

On the death of Conall, King of the Scots of Dalriada (Argyll and the adjoining Isles), so great was the authority acquired by St. Columba through his personality and royal connections, that it fell to him to designate Conall's successor on the throne. Adamnan tells of the angelical visitations to the Saint whilst staying on Hinba, which led him to summon Conall's cousin, Aidan, to Iona, and there " ordain " him King by the laying on of hands. (This is the earliest record of a royal hallowing in Britain.)

Aidan was the ancestor of the early kings of Scotland, the majority of whom were buried in Iona; an ancestor, too, through the Stuarts, of the reigning House of Windsor.

This prayer, which is preserved in the Leofric Missal, is believed to have been used by Columba at Aidan's consecration. (See Scottish Coronations, by John, Marquess of Bute.)

O Lord, who from everlasting governest the Kingdom of the Kings, bless thou this ruling prince, and glorify him with such a blessing that he may hold the sceptre of salvation and be found rich with the gifts of sanctifying mercy. Grant unto him by Thine inspiration even so to rule the people in meekness, as Thou didst cause Solomon to obtain a kingdom of peace. May he ever be subject unto Thee in fear, and fight for Thee in quietness; may he be protected by Thy shield and remain ever a conqueror without a combat. And grant Thou that the nations may keep faith with him, that his nobles may have peace and love charity. May he hold from Thee a strong seat of government, that with gladness and righteousness he may glory in an eternal kingdom, which do Thou Thyself be pleased to grant, who livest and reignest with the Eternal Father, together with the Holy Ghost, one God for ever and ever. Amen.

THE *ALTUS* OF COLUMBA

" *Of (Columba's) Latin hymns only three remain. They are preserved in the Liber Hymnorum, a MS. probably of the end of eleventh century, and are known as the ' Altus,' ' In Te Christo,' and ' Noli Pater.' No doubt exists as to the genuineness of the ' Altus.' It is the most famous of the three. . . . The poem takes its name from the first word, and each of its twenty-two stanzas begins in order with a letter of the alphabet, probably as a help to the memory. The poem has enjoyed a great reputation, and has been variously rendered into English.*"

Magnus Maclean: The Literature of the Celts

Only two verses are given here—the A and the R stanzas. In the latter, comments Dr. Maclean, we have a picture of the judgment not unlike the Dies Irae.

Ancient of Days; enthroned on high;
The Father unbegotten He,
Whom space containeth not nor time,
Who was and is and aye shall be;
And one-born Son and Holy Ghost,
Who co-eternal glory share.
One only God of Persons Three
We praise, acknowledge and declare.

Riseth the dawn—the day is near,
Day of the Lord, the King of Kings;
A day of wrath and vengeance just,
Of darkness, clouds and thunderings:
A day of anguish, cries and tears,
When glow of women's love shall pale;
When man shall cease to strive with man,
And all the world's desires shall fail.

Translated by the *Rev. Anthony Mitchell*

ERIN AND ALBA

THE SAINT SENDS A MESSAGE

I give thee my blessing to carry, fair Youth,
And my benediction over the sea,
One sevenfold half upon Erin in truth,
One half upon Alba the same to be.

Then take thee my blessing with thee to the west,
For my heart in my bosom is broken; I fail;
Should death of a sudden now pierce my breast,
I should die of the love that I bear the Gael.

From Columcille's *Ben Edar*
(Translated by Douglas Hyde)

ST. COLUMBA AND ST. MUNGO (KENTIGERN) MEET

(On one of his missionary journeys Columba was able to satisfy a long-felt desire to visit his unknown brother, Kentigern (better known as Mungo, the Beloved One), who had been trained at the school of St. Serf, in Fife, and had made his centre at Cathures, now Glasgow.)

And when the opportune moment came, the holy Columba went forth, and a great crowd of disciples and others accompanied him, desiring to behold and look upon the face of so great a man. And when he approached the place which is called Mellindenor, where the saint was then staying, he divided all his people into three bands, and sent a messenger before him to announce to the holy prelate his arrival, and that of those who were with him.

31

The holy bishop rejoiced at the things which were told him concerning them, and calling to him his clergy and people, he, in like manner, divided them into three bands, and went forward with spiritual songs to meet them. In the forefront of the procession were placed the juniors in order of time, next the more advanced in years, then with himself there walked those who had grown old in good days, white and hoary, venerable in countenance, gesture and bearing, yea, even in grey hairs. And all sang, " In the ways of the Lord, how great is the glory of the Lord." And again they answered, " The way of the just is made straight, and the path of the saints is prepared." On St. Columba's side they sang with tuneful voice, " Unto the God of gods everyone of them shall appear in Sion," with Alleulia.

. . . When these two godlike men met, they embraced and kissed each other, and having first satiated themselves with the spiritual banquet of Divine words, they refreshed themselves with bodily food.

. . . For some days these Saints passed the time together conversing on the things which are of God, and on those which belong to the salvation of souls . . . (Before bidding each other farewell) they exchanged pastoral staves in pledge and testimony of their mutual love in Christ.

Jocelin (a monk of Furness): Life of St. Kentigern

THE PASSING OF COLUMBA

THE SAINT REVEALS HIS APPROACHING END

One day in the month of May . . . the old man, weary with age, is borne on a wagon and goes to visit the Brethren while at their work. And while they are busy in the western part of the isle of Iona, he began on that day to speak thus: " During the Easter festival just over in April, ' with desire I have desired ' to pass away to Christ the Lord, as He had even granted to me if I liked. But, lest your festival of joy should be turned into sadness, I preferred that the day of my departure from the world should be put off a little longer."

The monks of his household were greatly afflicted whilst they heard these sad words of his, and he began to cheer them as far as he could with words of consolation. At the close of which, sitting just as he was in the wagon, turning his face eastward he blessed the island, with its islanders. . . . After those words of blessing the Saint is carried back to his monastery.

. . . At the end of the same week, that is on the Sabbath day [Saturday], he and his dutiful attendant, Diormit, go to bless the granary which was near by. And on entering it, when the Saint had blessed it and two heaps of corn stored up in it, he uttered these words with giving of thanks, saying: " Greatly do I congratulate the monks of my household that this year, also, if I should perchance have to depart from you, you will have enough for the year without stint." And hearing this word Diormit, the attendant, began to be sorrowful and to speak thus: " Often dost thou make us sad, Father, at this time of the year, because thou dost make mention so often of thy passing away." To whom the Saint made this answer: " I have a certain little secret chat to hold with thee, and if thou wilt firmly promise me to disclose it to no one before my death, I shall be able to tell thee something more clearly as to my going hence." And when the attendant, on bended knees, had finished making this promise according to the Saint's wish, the venerable man thereupon thus speaks: " In the Sacred Volumes this day is called the Sabbath, which is, interpreted, Rest. And this day is truly a Sabbath day for me, because it is for me the last day of this present laborious life, on which I rest after the fatigues of my labours; and this night, at midnight, when begins the solemn day of the Lord, according to the saying of the Scriptures, I shall go the way of my fathers. For already my Lord Jesus Christ deigns to invite me, to Whom, I say, in the middle of this night, He Himself inviting me, I shall depart. For so it has been revealed to me by the Lord Himself." Hearing these sad words, the attendant began to weep bitterly. And the Saint tried to console him as well as he could.

COLUMBA AND THE WHITE HORSE
After this the Saint goes out of the granary, and, returning to the monastery, sits down half-way at the place

where afterwards a cross, fixed in a mill-stone, and standing to this day, is to be seen at the roadside. And while the Saint, weary with age as I have said, rested there, sitting for a little while, behold the white horse, a faithful servant, runs up to him, the one which used to carry the milk pails to and fro between the byre and the monastery. He, coming up to the Saint, wonderful to tell, lays his head against his breast—inspired, as I believe, by God, by whose dispensation every animal has sense to perceive things according as its Creator Himself has ordained—knowing that His master was soon about to leave him, and that he would see him no more, began to whinny and to shed copious tears into the lap of the Saint. . . . And the attendant, seeing this, began to drive away the weeping mourner, but the Saint forbade him, saying: " Let him alone, let him alone, for he loves me. . . ." And so saying, he blessed his servant the horse as it sadly turned to go away from him.

THE SAINT BLESSES THE ISLAND

And then going and ascending the knoll that overlooks the monastery he stood for a little while on its top, and there standing and raising both hands he blessed his monastery, saying: " Upon this place, small though it be and mean, not only the kings of the Scotic people, with their peoples, but also the rulers of barbarous and foreign races, with the people subject to them, shall confer great and no common honour; by the Saints also even of other churches shall no common reverence be accorded to it."

HIS LAST HOURS

After these words, coming down from the knoll and returning to the monastery, he sat in his hut transcribing the Psalter; and coming to that verse of the thirty-third Psalm, where it is written: " But they that seek the Lord shall not want any good thing," " here," he says, " I must stop at the foot of this page, and what follows let Baithene write."

. . . After transcribing the verse at the end of the page, as above mentioned, the Saint enters the church for the vesper mass of the vigil of the Lord's Day, and as soon as this is over, he returns to his cell and sits up throughout the night on his bed, where he had the bare rock for pallet and a stone for pillow, which to this day stands by his grave as his monumental pillar. And so, there sitting up, he gives his last commands to the Brethren, his attendant alone hearing them, saying: " These my last words I commend to you, O my sons, that ye have mutual and unfeigned charity among yourselves, with peace: and if, according to the example of the holy Fathers, ye shall observe this, God, the Comforter of the good, will help you; and I, abiding with Him, will intercede for you; and not only will the necessaries of this present life be sufficiently supplied by Him, but the rewards of the good things of Eternity, prepared for those who keep His Divine commandments, shall also be bestowed."

HE BREATHES FORTH HIS SPIRIT

After which, as the happy last hour gradually approached, the Saint was silent. Then, when the bell began to toll at midnight, rising in haste he goes to the church, and running faster than the others he enters it alone, and on bended knees falls down in prayer at the altar. At the same moment Diormit, his attendant, who followed more slowly, sees from a distance the whole church filled within with Angelic light round about the Saint. And as he drew near to the door, the same light which he had seen suddenly withdrew, and this light a few others of the Brethren who stood afar off also saw. Diormit, therefore, entering the church, moans out with mournful voice, " Where art thou, Father?" And as the lights of the Brethren had not yet been brought in, groping his way in the dark he finds the Saint lying before the altar, and raising him up a little and sitting down by him he lays the holy head on his bosom. And meanwhile the community of monks, running up with lights, began to weep at the sight of their dying Father. And as we have learned from some who were there present the Saint, his soul not yet departing, with open eyes upturned, looked round about on either side with wonderful cheerfulness and joy of countenance on seeing the holy Angels coming to meet him. Diormit then lifts up the holy right hand of the Saint that he may bless the choir of monks. But the venerable Father himself at

35

the same time moved his hand as much as he was able, so that what was impossible for him to do with his voice at his soul's departure he might still do by the movement of his hand, namely, give his blessing to the Brethren. And after thus signifying his holy benediction, immediately breathed forth his spirit. And it having left the tabernacle of the body, the face remained so ruddy and wonderfully gladdened by the vision of the Angels that it seemed not to be that of one dead, but of one living and sleeping. Meanwhile, the whole church resounded with sorrowful wailings.

THE OBSEQUIES

Meanwhile, after the departure of his holy soul, the matin hymns being ended, the sacred body is carried with melodious psalmody from the church to the house whence, a little while before, he had come alive; and for three days and as many nights his honourable obsequies are performed with due observance. And these being ended with sweet praises of God, the venerable body of our holy and blessed patron, wrapped in a fair shroud and placed in the tomb prepared for it, is buried with due reverence, to rise again in resplendent and eternal brightness.

Adamnan: Life of St. Columba

ON THE DEATH OF COLUMCILLE

The bitter drink of herbs whose healing's gone;
   The failed right arm, the stiff and marrowless bone;
The harp that hath for heart's responsion—none:
   Such are we since he fell—our noblest one.

*Dallan the Bard** (Translated by E. R.)

HIS GRACE—HIS SOUL—HIS BODY

In the old Irish life of St. Columba, written a thousand years ago and handed down to us in the *Leabhar Breac*, there are quoted the following lines upon St. Columba, made by St. Brechan:—

His grace in Hii (Iona) without stain,
And his soul in Derry;
And his body under the flagstone
Under which are Brigid and Patrick.

Columba's contemporary and head of the Order of the Bards.

36

These three places—Iona, Derry and Down—together constitute the " full habitation " of the saint.

To Iona, his beloved island home during the years of his great missionary enterprise, he gives his " stainless rgace."

To Derry, where in the year 546 he founded his best-loved church, he gives his " soul "; " for he loved that city very much," says his old biographer. " As he said:—

> The reason why I love Derry is
> Its quietness, its purity;
> For 'tis full of angels white
> From one end to the other."

To Down his body is believed to have been eventually taken, and there interred beside those of St. Patrick and St. Brigit or Bride.* These three great saints of Ireland—the first Irish only by adoption—are symbolised in the triple-leaved shamrock, the national and spiritual symbol of that country. In the sixteenth century, however, Lord Grey, Deputy Governor of Ireland in 1536-7, in his zeal for the destruction of religious houses and for the establishment of Henry VIII as head of the Church in Ireland, gave the ancient church of Down to the flames.

" He rode to the north," says Holinshed, " and in this journey he razed St. Patrick, his church in Downe, and burnt the monuments of Patrick, Brigide and Colme (Columba), who are said to have been there interred. . . . This fact lost him sundry hearts in that country, always after detesting the King and Council."

Grey was eventually arraigned and tried in London, and was executed on Tower Hill in 1541.

THE RUNE OF COLUMCILLE

Hear ye my Rune from the blue deeps of far days,
  Sang and flushed Iona's heart;
Columkeel hath the keen eye of eagle,
  So to seek the noon-tide of nine rays.

* " But this is totally denied by the Scots, who affirm that the contrary is shewn in a life of the saint, extracted out of the Pope's library, and translated out of the Latin into Erse, by father Cal-o horan which decided in favour of Iona, the momentous dispute."—*Pennant.*

Hear ye my Rune from the blue deeps of far days,
  Sang and throbbed Iona's heart;
Columkeel hath the strong back of elk-stag,
  So to bear all our people's burdens.

Hear ye my Rune from the blue deeps of far days,
  Sang and thrill'd Iona's heart;
Columkeel hath the soft hand of woman,
  So to soothe the sore wounds of bruised ones.

Kenneth Macleod

A SEVENTH CENTURY PORTRAIT

Saint Columba was born of noble parentage. . . . In the forty-second year of his age, desiring to make a pilgrimage from Ireland to Britain, he sailed forth. And he, who even from boyhood had been devoted to the school of Christ and the study of wisdom, preserving by the gift of God integrity of body and purity of soul, showed that although placed upon earth he was fitted for a heavenly life. For he was angelic of aspect, clean in speech, holy in deed, of excellent disposition, great in counsel, for thirty-four years trained as an Island-soldier (of Christ). He could not pass the space even of a single hour without applying himself either to prayer, or reading, or writing, or to some manual labour. By day and by night he was so occupied, without any intermission, in unwearied exercises of fasts and vigils that the burden of any one of these particular labours might seem to be beyond human endurance. And, amid all, dear to all, ever showing a pleasant, holy countenance, he was gladdened in his inmost heart by the joy of the Holy Spirit.   *Adamnan:* Life of St. Columba

A TWENTIETH CENTURY PORTRAIT

Altogether he was a remarkable man. Tall, well-featured, with long hair falling to each shoulder from the temples (for the early Celtic priests shaved the front of their heads), he had a commanding presence, and was, in fact, full of a restless energy, passionate and impetuous. He had that quality of voice which does not appear to be raised when speaking to those at hand and which yet can be heard clearly at a distance. A statesman, an organiser, he was almost continuously on the move, over land, by sea, daring any peril, unsparing of himself, teaching, converting, founding, succeeding.

He succeeded very well indeed—so well that his own folk, the Gaels or Scots (Ireland is called Scotia in the old records), who landed, as he landed, on the Argyllshire part of Scotland, managed in time to give their kings to Scotland, their tongue, and their particular methods of church government. All that was distinctive of the ancient Pictish Scotland, strong enough in its time to repel the Romans, faded away before this Columban energy and statesmanship, leaving scarcely a trace behind. It is the great mystery in Scottish history, that to this day scholars debate the identity of the Picts, what tongue they spoke and how they were governed in church and state. Statesmanship that is so successful has doubtless its own reward, even if suspicion of doubtful dealings be not inevitably aroused. In any case, I was inclined to be one of those who felt no great urge to pay further tribute to Columba and Iona; who in fact would rather learn somewhat more of our real forebears, the Picts, and give his proper place to that Ninian who was a missionary in Scotland one hundred and fifty years before Columba arrived.

. . . In a word, I was prepared to be prejudiced to the hilt against Columba. But, unfortunately, Iona is the last place in the world to help a prejudice. If one doesn't forget it, at least one cannot be bothered with it for the moment, not in the rain, in the soft air.

. . . For one can also see that other half of Columba's character, the affectionate part, full of warmth and understanding. It had the nobility from which, perhaps, all his restless energy received direction. Tolerance, temperance, kindness, simplicity, obedience, forgiveness—we know the rules that governed their lives; but, above all, from their religion they got the conception of charity, of love. It is the ancient goodness of the human heart, the primordial goodness. And a religion that enshrines it will always persist. Those who have this goodness in them are aware of life in the same way as they are aware of light. Truly, life itself is an inner light.

And, at its best, it is a universal light. Columba loved the birds, and the white horse that carried the farm produce bore Columba a special affection. Indeed, as Adamnan relates . . . the white horse wept on taking leave of its dying master. Which may be an exaggeration of the truth; but still—of the truth. And that wise and scholarly men of his age believed it to be the simple truth shows at least what they wanted to believe. Which is the essence of the matter. Beyond miracle and morality and theology, they desired this goodness. And kings and priests and murderers and perverts of all kinds went to Columba in Iona to find again the peace of that goodness.

The most remarkable thing I discovered in Adamnan's remarkable record is this preoccupation with light as the manifestation or symbol of goodness. The miracles are the light in legendary form. And many of them—particularly those relating to prevision or " second sight "—may not be so legendary as all that.

The simplest and perhaps the best expression of this conjunction of light and goodness may be found in the story of that which happened to the brethren on their return to the monastery after toiling all day in the fields on the west side of the island. When half-way home with their burdens, each had felt within him " something wonderful and unusual " but had not cared to confess it, until at last it could no longer be hid, and one tried to express it thus: " I perceive some fragrance of wondrous odour, as of that of all flowers collected into one; also some burning as of fire, not penal but somehow very sweet; moreover, also a certain unaccustomed gladness diffused in my heart, which suddenly consoles me in a wonderful manner, and gladdens me to such a degree that I can remember no more the sadness, nor any labour. Yea, even the load, though a heavy one, which I am carrying on my back from this place to the monastery, is so lightened, I know not how, that I do not perceive I have a load at all."

Columba, "mindful of their labours," had sent his spirit to meet their steps.

Gladness, then, is the keynote of the experience.

Adamnan knew of it in its many manifestations, and at one point writes: "St. Columba, as he himself did not deny . . . in some contemplations of divine grace beheld even the whole world as if gathered together in one ray of the sun, gazing on it as manifested before him, while his inmost soul was enlarged in a wonderful manner."

Neil M. Gunn: Off in a Boat

COLUMBA'S SECOND-SIGHT

For one thing of great Gaelic import, Columba has been given a singular pre-eminence—because (so it is averred) he was the first of our race of whom is recorded the systematic use of the strange gift of spiritual foresight, "second-sight." It has been stated authoritatively that he is the first of whom there is record as having possessed this faculty; but that could only be averred by one ignorant of ancient Gaelic literature. Even in Adamnan's chronicle, within some seventy years after the death of Columba, there is record of others having this faculty, apart from the perhaps more purely spiritual vision of his mother Aithne, when an angel raimented her with the beauty of her unborn son; or of his foster-father, the priest Cruithnechan, who saw the singular light of the soul about his sleeping pupil; or of the Abbot Brendan, who redeemed the saint from excommunication and perhaps death by his vision of him advancing with a pillar of fire before him and an angel on either side. (When, long years afterwards, Brendan died in Ireland, Colum in Iona startled his monks by calling for an immediate celebration of the Eucharist, because it had been revealed to him that St. Brendan had gone to the heavenly fatherland yesternight: "Angels came to meet his soul: I saw the whole earth illumined with their glory.") Among others there is the story of the Abbot Kenneth, who, sitting at supper, rose so suddenly as to leave without his sandals, and at the altar of his church prayed for Colum, at that moment in dire peril upon the sea; the story of Ernan, who, fishing in the river Fenda, saw the death of Colum in a symbol of

41

flame; the story of Lugh mac Tailchan, who, at Cloinfinchoil, beheld Iona (which he had never visited) and above it a blaze of angels' wings, and Colum's soul. In the most ancient tales there is frequent allusion to what we call second-sight.

. . . There is something strangely beautiful in most of these " second-sight " stories of Columba. The faculty itself is so apt to the spiritual law that one wonders why it is so set apart in doubt. It would, I think, be far stranger if there were no such faculty.

That, I believe, it were needless to say, were it not that these words may be read by many to whom this quickened inward vision is a superstition, or a fantastic glorification of insight. I believe; not only because there is nothing too strange for the soul, whose vision surely I will not deny, while I accept what is lesser, the mind's prescience, and, what is least, the testimony of the eyes. . . . Spiritual logic demands it.

. . . I would as little, however, deny that this inward vision is sometimes imperfect and untrustworthy, as I would assert that it is infallible. . . . When it is in truth a spiritual vision, then we are in company of what is the essential life, that which we call divine.

It was this that Columba had, this serene perspicuity. That it was a conscious possession we know from his own words, for he gave this answer to one who marvelled: " Heaven has granted to some to see on occasion in their mind, clearly and surely, the whole of earth and sea and sky."

Fiona Macleod: Iona

THE TONGUE TELLING WONDERS

To the eye of sinless-hearted Colmcille
Godhead gave the seeing nothing stayed;
In his tongue he stowed reports of the unbegotten
Deeds of the days unborn; in his calloused hand
Currents of the governed good world to arrange them
As was fit, so His purposes be served.
And through-seeing and foreseeing and power-plying
Made Alba an eyrie of the Lord.

Robert Farren: The First Exile

42

THE COLUMBAN CHURCH AND AFTER

THIS WE KNOW FOR CERTAIN

This we know for certain, that he (Columba) left successors renowned for their continency, their love of God, and observance of monastic rites. It is true they followed uncertain rules in their observance of the great festival, as having none to bring them the synodal decrees for the observance of Easter, by reason of their being so far away from the rest of the world; wherefore they only practised such works of piety and chastity as they could learn from the prophetical, evangelical, and apostolical writings.

Bede (ob. 735): Ecclesiastical History

THE WINDS BLOW A WELCOME GUEST TO IONA

(Adamnan) wrote a book upon the Holy Places, of great service to many readers: its author, by information and dictation, was Arcwulf, a bishop of Gaul, who for the sake of the Holy Places had gone to Jerusalem, and after travelling through all the Promised Land, had visited Damascus, Constantinople, Alexandria, and many islands of the sea. And returning again by ship to his own land, he was carried by violent storms to the west coast of Britain; and after many adventures came to the said servant of

Christ, Adamnan.* There he was found to be a man learned in the Scriptures and acquainted with the Holy Places, and was very gladly received by him and more gladly heard, wherefore all worthy of mention that he testified he had seen in the Holy Places, Adamnan was at pains to set down in writing.†

Bede: Ecclesiastical History

THE MISSION TO THE ANGLES

From the aforesaid island (Iona) and college of monks, was Aidan sent to instruct the English nation in Christ.

. . . It is reported that when King Oswald‡ (of Northumbria) had asked a bishop of the Scots to administer the word of faith to him and his nation there was first sent to him another man of more austere disposition, who, meeting with no success, and being unregarded by the English people, returned home, and in an assembly of the elders reported that he had not been able to do any good to the nation he had been sent to preach to, because they were uncivilized men and of a stubborn and barbarous disposition. They, as is testified, in a great council seriously debated what was to be done, being desirous that the nation should receive the salvation it demanded, and grieving that they had not received the preacher sent to them. Then said

* Adamnan became Abbot of Iona in 679.

† " (At Iona) in the long winter evenings he told his story to appreciative listeners, the Abbot wrote down his descriptions quickly on waxed tablets, and afterwards made a copy on parchment, and Arculf drew plans for him of the Church of the Holy Sepulchre and three other famous churches, which are reproduced in the edition of the work in Migne's *Patrologia.* Arculf's stories about St. George, which he ' learned in the city of Constantinople from some well-informed citizens,' show that the great martyr's fame reached Iona centuries before the English army took him for their patron saint."—*E. C. Trenholme:* The Story of Iona.

‡ Oswald, the rightful heir to the throne (of Northumbria), was converted to Christianity when a political refugee in Scotland, and Iona itself was almost certainly the place of his baptism.— *Rev. E. C. Trenholme:* The Story of Iona.

Aidan,* who was also present in the council, to the priest then spoken of, " I am of opinion, brother, that you were more severe to your unlearned hearers than you ought to have been, and did not at first, conformably to the apostolic rule, give them the milk of more easy doctrine, till being by degrees nourished with the word of God, they should be capable of great perfection, and be able to practise God's sublimer precepts."

Having heard these words, all present began diligently to weigh what had been said, and presently concluded that he deserved to be made a bishop and ought to be sent to instruct the incredulous and unlearned; since he was found to be endued with singular discretion, which is the mother of other virtues, and accordingly being ordained, they sent him to their friend King Oswald, to preach; and he, as time proved, afterwards appeared to possess all other virtues, as well as the discretion for which he was before remarkable.

Bede: Ecclesiastical History

A GREAT IONA MISSIONARY

ST. AIDAN, BISHOP OF LINDISFARNE

I have written these things of the person and works of Aidan, by no means approving of his imperfect knowledge of the keeping of Easter†—indeed, disapproving of it very strongly—but as a truthful historian recounting frankly the things which he did, or caused to be done, and praising

* St. Aidan was consecrated bishop and dispatched on his mission in 635. He built a monastery on Lindisfarne (Holy Island), off the Northumberland coast, which became the headquarters of the Celtic Church in England. He preached to the people in Gaelic at first, whilst King Oswald sat at his feet interpreting into the Anglian dialect. (See *E. C. Trenholme, op. cit.*)

† In Aidan's time the Columban Church still calculated the date of Easter by a formula which had been discarded by the Church on the Continent.

those of his deeds which are worthy of praise . . . the cultivation of peace and charity, of continence and of humility; a mind that was victor over anger and greed, and scorned pride and boasting; faithful keeping, as teaching, of the divine commandments; constant study and vigil; authority becoming to a bishop, in stripping pretension from the proud and powerful and in comforting the sick; and mercy in helping or defending the poor. And—to sum many things in a few words—as far as we have learnt from those who knew him, he endeavoured to neglect none of all those things which in the Gospel, or the writings of the Prophets and Apostles, he had learned should be done, but to fulfil them, to his best strength, in works. These things in the said Bishop I greatly prize and love, since I doubt not that they were truly pleasing to God.

Bede: Ecclesiastical History

COMMENTS AND TRIBUTES

The first great monasteries of Ireland were nothing else, to speak simply, than clans re-organized under a religious form.

Montalembert: The Monks of the West

Few forms of Christianity have offered an ideal of Christian perfection so pure as the Celtic Church of the sixth, seventh and eighth centuries. Nowhere, perhaps, has God been better worshipped in spirit than in those great monastic communities of Hy or Iona, of Bangor, of Clonard, or of Lindisfarne.

Ernest Renan

Charlemagne knew and reverenced " this little people of Iona."

Fiona Macleod: Note to Iona

Of these splendid traditions, of this bright example, of these evangelistic triumphs you are the heirs. . . . While all else changes the spirit is unchanged. The simplicity, the self-devotion, the prayerfulness, the burning love of

Christ which shone forth in those Celtic missionaries of old must be your spiritual equipment now.

Bishop Lightfoot: Leaders in the Northern Church

MAGNUS BARELEGS VISITS IONA

In 1097, King Magnus of Norway (called Magnus Barelegs because of his adoption of the kilt during his long operations in the Hebrides) on a triumphal tour of his new territories, anchored his war-galleys in the Sound of Mull and came ashore to do homage to the Isle of Columba.

King Magnus came with all his host to the holy island, and gave there quarter and peace to all men, and to the household of all men. Men say this, that he wished to open the small church of Columcille; and the King did not go in, but closed the door again immediately, and immediately locked it, and said that none should be so daring as to go into that church; and thenceforward it has been so done.

Then King Magnus proceeded south to Islay, (and) plundered and burned there.*

Heimskringla, Magnus Barelegs' Saga

A SACRILEGIOUS MARAUDER

In 1509, Alan Macrory, chief of Clanranald, who had fought against the Lord of the Isles at Bloody Bay, was tried and hanged before the King at Blair Atholl, in punishment for his evil deeds. He is commemorated in a contemporary poem preserved in the Book of the Dean of Lismore:—

The one demon of the Gael is dead,
A tale 'tis well to remember,
Fierce ravager of church and cross.

* Magnus . . . an unpeaceful man, who thirsted after others' possessions and thought little of his own, he infested Scotia and Cornubia (Wales) . . . practising piracy.—*Theodoric:* Historia de Antiquitate Regum Norwagiensium.

Thou hast—not thine only crime—
Ravaged I and Reilig Odhrain;
Fiercely didst thou then destroy
Preiest's vestments and vessels for the mass.

At the time thou first mad'st war
There was the abbot's horrid corpse,

Besides that other lawless raid
Against Finan in Glengarry.

'Tis no wonder thou didst keep
Far away, Alan, from the gallows.

Translated from the Gaelic of
Red Finlay the Bard

THE LIBRARY

The monastery was the repository of most of the antient Scotch records. The library here must also have been invaluable, if we can depend upon Boethius, who asserts that Fergus II, assisting Alaric the Goth in the sacking of Rome, brought away as share of the plunder a chest of books, which he presented to the monastery of Iona. Aeneas Sylvius (afterwards Pope Pius II) intended, when he was in Scotland, to have visited the library in search of lost books of Livy, but was prevented by the death of the King, James I. A small parcel of them was in 1525 taken to Aberdeen, and great pains taken to unfold them, but through age and the tenderness of the parchment, little could be read: but from what the learned were able to make out, the work appeared by the style to have rather been a fragment of Sallust than of Livy. But the register and records of the island, all written on parchment, and probably the more antique and valuable remains, were all destroyed by that worse than Gothic Synod* which at the Reformation declared war against all science.

Pennant: Voyage to the Hebrides (1772)

* The Synod of Argyll.

THE BELLS OF IONA

Letter, King Charles I to the Bishop of Rapho, desiring him to restore to the Bishop of the Isles two of the bells of Icolmkill that had been taken from Icolmkill to Rapho by Bishop Knox, 1635.

Reverend Father in God: Whereas we ar informed that Andro late Bischop of Rapho at his transportatioun from the Bischoprik of Yles did without just cause or aney warrant frome our late royall father or us, carie with him *tuo of the principal bells that wer in Icolmkill* and place them in some of the Churches of Rapho; To which purpois we doe remember that at the tyme of your being Beschop of Yles yow wer a sutter to us for effectuating that thing at your predicessour the Bischop of Raphoes hands which we now requyre of yow: Therefor and in regard we have gevin ordour to THE PRESENT BISCHOP OF YLES for repairing the Cathedrall Church of that Bischoprik, and that it is fit for such things as do properlie belong thereunto be restored; it is our plesour *that you caus delyver unto the said Bischop these tuo Bells* for the use of the said Cathedrall Church with such tymlie convenience as may be; Which we will acknowledge as acceptable service done unto us.— Whythall, 14 March 1635.

From *Collectanea de Rebus Albanicis*

CHARLES I PLANS TO RESTORE THE CATHEDRAL CHURCH

Letter, Charles I to the Lords of Exchequer, directing the payment of a grant of four hundred pounds sterling to the Bishop of the Isles, for repairing the Cathedral Church of Icolmkill; and warrant of the said Lords following thereupon, 1635.

Right trusty and right welbeloved Cousins and Counsellouris; right trusty and right welbeloved Counsellouris; and trusty and welbeloved; Wee greete yow well. Whereas the reverend father in God the BISCHOPE OF ILES *is by oure direction to repayre the*

Cathedrall Church of Icolmkill, the doeing whereof in such manner as is requisite will requyre (as we are credibly informed) greate paynes and charges which he cannot possibly undergoe without oure assistance and helpe. Therefore and in reguard it is a work which wee affect Wee have thought fitt to allowe unto him and his Assignes *the sume of Fower hundred pounds Sterlin* for the more ready payment whereof wee doe hereby require and authorise yow to assign him and them to all the few dewties payeable unto us by SIR LAUCHLANE McCLEANE till the sayd sume be compleately payed, the first termes payment whereof to be at Martimasse next 1635. And in the meanetyme that yow be carefull that he goe on with the sayd reparatioun, authorising him with full power to requyre service of all such persones in these parts as doe owe the same unto us, and that for carrying and transporting of commodities unto that worke; for doeing of all which these presents shall be unto yow and every one of yow a sufficient warrant; from our Court at Whythall the 10 day of Merche 1635.

Addressed Thus

To our right trustie and right welbeloved Cousins and Counsellouris to our right trustie and welbeloved Counsellouris and to our trustie and welbeloved Counsellouris The Earles Morton and Traquhair our Treasurers principall and Duputie of our Kingdome of Scotland, and to the remanent Earles, Lords, and other Comissioneris of Exchequer of our said Kingdome.

Apud Ed primo July 1635

The Lordis ordaynes the lettre to be registrat for warrandeing the Thessauraris principall and deputie for payeing the lyk sowme yerely to the Bischope at the termes the said few dwetye is payable ay and whill he be payit of the sowme of 4c lib said.*

(Sic subscribitur) TRAQUAIRE I.P.D.

From *Collectanea de Rebus Albanicis*

* " The great political troubles leading up to the Civil War broke out soon afterwards, and must have put an end to such projects."—*E. C. Trenholme:* The Story of Iona.

RUNES, INVOCATIONS, AND PRAYERS

BLESSING OF THE HOUSE

May God give blessing
      To the house that is here.
May Jesus give blessing
      To the house that is here.
May Spirit give blessing
      To the house that is here.
May the Three give blessing
      To the house that is here.
May Brigit give blessing
      To the house that is here.
May Michael give blessing
      To the house that is here.
May Mary give blessing
      To the house that is here.
May Columba give blessing
      To the house that is here.
May the King of the Elements
      Be its help
      The King of Glory
            Have charge upon it.

Christ the Beloved,
      Son of Mary Virgin,
      And the gentle Spirit
            Be pouring therein.

51

Michael, bright warrior
King of the angels,
Watch and ward it
With the power of his sword.

And Brigit, the fair and tender,
Her hue like the cotton grass,
Rich tressed maiden
Of ringlets of gold.

Mary, the fair and tender,
Be nigh the hearth,
And Columba kindly
Giving benediction
In fulfilment of each promise
On those within,
On those within.

Alexander Carmichael: Carmina Gadelica

HYMN OF THE PROCESSION

On the first day of May, the people of the croft townland are up betimes and busy as bees about to swarm. This is the day of the migrating from townland to moorland, from the winter homestead to the summer sheiling. . . . All the families of the townland bring their different flocks together at a particular place and drive the whole away. . . . All who meet them on the way bless the triall (procession) and invoke upon it a good day, much luck and prosperity, and the safe shepherding of the Son of Mary on man and beast.

Valiant Michael of the white steeds,
Who subdued the Dragon of blood,
For love of God, for pains of Mary's Son,
Spread thy wing over us, shield us all,
Spread thy wing over us, shield us all.

Mary beloved! Mother of the White Lamb,
Shield, oh shield us, pure Virgin of nobleness,
And Bride the beauteous, shepherdess of the flocks,
Safeguard thou our cattle, surround us together,
    Safeguard thou our cattle, surround us together.

And Columba, beneficent, benign,
In name of Father, and of Son, and of Spirit Holy,
Through the Three-in-One, through the Trinity,
Encompass thou ourselves, shield our procession,
    Encompass thou ourselves, shield our procession.

O Father! O Son! O Spirit Holy!
Be the Triune with us day and night,
On the machair plain or on the mountain ridge
Be the Triune with us and His arm around our head,
    Be the Triune with us and His arm around our head!*
                Alexander Carmichael: Carmina Gadelica

COLUMBA'S HERDING

May the herding of Columba
Encompass you going and returning,
Encompass you in strath and on ridge,
    And on the edge of each rough region.

May it keep you from pit and from mire,
Keep you from hill and from crag,
Keep you from loch and from downfall,
    Each evening and each darkling.

May it keep you from the mean destroyer,
Keep you from the mischievous niggard,
Keep you from the mishap of bar-stumbling
    And from the untoward fays.

* This is the hymn as sung in Benbecula, South Uist and Barra,
where Roman Catholicism prevails. In Lewis, Harris and North
Uist the people confine their invocations to the Trinity.

The peace of Columba be yours in the grazing,
The peace of Brigit be yours in the grazing,
The peace of Mary be yours in the grazing,
And may you return home safe-guarded.

Alexander Carmichael: Carmina Gadelica

HERDING BLESSING

Mary Mother, tend thou the offspring all,
Bride of the fair palms, guard thou my flocks,
Kindly Columba, thou saint of many powers,
Encompass thou the breeding cows, bestow on me herds,
Kindly Columba, thou saint of many powers,
Encompass thou the breeding cows, bestow on me herds.

Alexander Carmichael: Carmina Gadelica

MILKING SONG

Come, Mary, and milk my cow,
Come, Bride, and encompass her,
Come, Columba, the benign,
And twine thine arms around my heifer.
Ho my heifer, ho my gentle heifer,
Ho my heifer, ho my gentle heifer,
Ho my heifer, ho my gentle heifer,
My heifer dear, generous and kind,
For the sake of the High King take to thy calf.

Alexander Carmichael: Carmina Gadelica

A BLESSING ON THE BOAT

At mouth of day,
The hour of buds,
Stood Columba
On the great white strand:
" O King of Storms,
Home sail the boat
From far away:
Thou King on High,
Home sail the boat! "

Kenneth Macleod

54

OCEAN BLESSING

Sea prayers and sea hymns were common amongst the seafarers of the Western Islands. Probably these originated with the early Celtic missionaries, who constantly traversed in their frail skin coracles the storm-swept, strongly tidal seas of those Hebrid Isles, oft and oft sealing their devotion with their lives.

Before embarking on a journey the voyagers stood round their boat and prayed to the God of the elements for a peaceful voyage over the stormy sea. The steersman led the appeal, while the swish of the waves below, the sough of the sea beyond, and the sound of the wind around blended with the voices of the suppliants and lent dignity and solemnity to the scene.

There are many small oratories round the West Coast where chiefs and clansmen were wont to pray before and after voyaging.   *A. C.*

O Thou who pervadest the heights,
Imprint on us Thy gracious blessing,
Carry us over the surface of the sea,
Carry us safely to a haven of peace,
Bless our boatmen and our boat,
Bless our anchors and our oars,
Each stay and halyard and traveller;
Our mainsails to our tall masts,
Keep, O King of the Elements, in their place
That we may return home in peace;
I myself will sit down at the helm,
It is God's own Son who will give me guidance,
As He gave to Columba the mild
What time he set stay to sails.

       Alexander Carmichael: Carmina Gadelica

ST. COLUMBA'S PLANT

St. John's Wort is one of the few plants still cherished by the people to ward away second sight, enchantment, witchcraft, evil eye and death, and to ensure peace and plenty in the house, increase and prosperity in the fold, and growth and fruition in the field. The plant is secretly secured in the bodices of the women and in the vests of the men, under the left armpit.

St. John's Wort, however, is effective only when the plant is accidentally found. When this occurs, the joy of the finder is great.

. . . There is a tradition among the people that Saint Columba carried the plant on his person because by his love and admiration for him who went about preaching Christ, and baptizing the converted, clothed in a garment of camel's hair and fed upon locusts and wild honey.   *A. C.*

I will pluck what I meet,
As in communion with my saint,
To stop the wiles of wily men,
And the arts of foolish women.

I will pluck Columba's plant
As a prayer to my King,
That mine be the power of Columba's plant
Over every one I see.

I will pluck the leaf above,
As ordained of the High King,
In name of the Three of Glory,
And of Mary, Mother of Christ.
    Alexander Carmichael: Carmina Gadelica

ST. COLUMBA'S DAY

The Gaels dedicated Thursday to St. Columba, as the Anglo Saxons (and others) dedicated it to Thor. " It was a lucky day for all enterprises—for warping thread, for beginning a pilgrimage, or any other undertaking," says Alexander Carmichael.

Thursday of Columba benign,
Day to send sheep on prosperity,
Day to send cow on calf,
Day to put the web in the warp.

Day to put coracle on the brine,
Day to place the staff to the flag,
Day to bear, day to die,
Day to hunt the heights.

Day to put horses in harness,
Day to send herds to pasture,
Day to make prayer efficacious,
Day of my beloved, the Thursday,
Day of my beloved, the Thursday.
Alexander Carmichael: Carmina Gadelica

FESTIVAL OF ST. COLUMBA
(*9th June*)

On St. Columba's Day, as for other festivals, oblation cakes were ritually baked in the Isles.

On Thursday eve the mother of a family made a bere, rye, or oaten cake into which she put a small silver coin. The cake was toasted before a fire of rowan, yew, oak, or other sacred wood. On the morning of Thursday the father took a keen-cutting knife and cut the cake into as many sections as there were children in the family, all the sections being equal. All the pieces were then placed in a *ciosan*—a bee-hive basket—and each child blindfold drew a piece of cake from the basket in name of the Father, Son and Spirit. The child who got the coin got the crop of lambs for the year. This was called *sealbh uan*—lamb luck. Sometimes it was arranged that the person who got the coin got a certain number of the lambs, and the others the rest of the lambs amongst them. Each child had a separate mark, and there was much emulation as to who had most lambs, the best lambs, and who took best care of the lambs.
Alexander Carmichael: Carmina Gadelica

In St. Kilda, all the milk in the community was delivered to the steward or his deputy on St. Columba's Day that it might be equally distributed among every man, woman and child on the island, " after the manner of the *agapae* or love feasts of early times."
George Seton: St. Kilda

PEACE

The peace of God, the peace of men,
The peace of Columba kindly,
The peace of Mary mild, the loving,
The peace of Christ, King of Tenderness,
    The peace of Christ, King of Tenderness.
Be upon each window, upon each door,
Upon each hole that lets in the light,
Upon the four corners of my house,
Upon the four corners of my bed,
    Upon the four corners of my bed;

Upon each thing my eye takes in,
Upon each thing my mouth takes in,
Upon my body that is of earth,
And upon my soul that came from on high,
    Upon my body that is of earth,
    And upon my soul that came from on high.

Alexander Carmichael: Carmina Gadelica

THE HEALING PEACE

The eolas of healing that Alan Dall, the blind poet, put upon the amadan (fool), touching the brow and the heart as he said here and here.

Deep peace I breathe into you,
O weariness, here:
O ache, here!
Deep peace, a soft white dove to you;
Deep peace, a quiet rain to you;
Deep peace, an ebbing wave to you!

Deep peace, red wind of the east to you;
Deep peace, grey wind of the west to you;
Deep peace, dark wind of the north to you;
Deep peace, blue wind of the south to you!

Deep peace, pure red of the flame to you;
Deep peace, pure white of the moon to you;
Deep peace, pure green of the grass to you;
Deep peace, pure brown of the earth to you;
Deep peace, pure grey of the dew to you;
Deep peace, pure blue of the sky to you!

Deep peace of the running wave to you;
Deep peace of the flowing air to you;
Deep peace of the quiet earth to you;
Deep peace of the sleeping stones to you;
Deep peace of the Yellow Shepherd to you;
Deep peace of the Wandering Shepherdess to you;
Deep peace from the flock of stars to you!

Deep peace from the Son of Peace,
Deep peace from the heart of Mary to you,
    And from Bridget of the Mantle
        Deep peace, deep peace!
    And with the kindness, too, of the Haughty Father
        Peace!
    In the name of the Three who are One,
        Peace!
And by the will of the King of the Elements,
        Peace, Peace!

(By the time the recitation of the *eolas* was finished, God had
healed the Amadan.)

Alan Dall, translated by *Fiona Macleod*

COLLECT FOR THE FEAST OF ST. COLUMBA

(CHURCH OF ROME)

Cordibus nostris, quaesumus Domine, coelestis gloriae
inspira desiderium et praesta ut in dextris illuc feramus
manipulos justitiae, ubi tecum coruscat Abbas Columba—
Per Dominum Jesum Christum, qui tecum vivit et regnat in
unitate Spiritus Sancti, Deus, per omnia saecula saeculorum.

                                Amen.

Breathe into our hearts, we beseech Thee, O Lord, a desire for Heavenly Glory, and grant that, carrying in our right hand the sheaves of justice, we may reach that place where shines with Thee, the Holy Abbot Columba— Through Jesus Christ our Lord, who liveth and reigneth with Thee in the unity of the Holy Spirit, God, world without end.

Amen.

COLLECT FOR THE FEASTS OF SS. KENTIGERN, PATRICK, COLUMBA AND NINIAN

O God, Who by the preaching of Thy blessed servant St. (Columba) didst cause the light of the Gospel to shine in this our land (*or* in these islands), grant, we beseech Thee, that having his life and labours in remembrance we may shew forth our thankfulness unto Thee for the same by following the example of his zeal and patience; through Jesus Christ our Lord. Amen.

From the *Prayer Book* of the Scottish Episcopal Church

A PRAYER FOR THE IONA COMMUNITY
(CHURCH OF SCOTLAND)

O God our Father Who didst give unto Thy servant, Columba, the gifts of courage, faith and cheerfulness and didst send men forth from Iona to carry the Word of Thine Evangel to every creature; grant we beseech Thee a like Spirit to Thy Church in Scotland, even at this present time. Further in all things the purpose of the New Community that hidden things may be revealed to them and new ways found to touch the hearts of men. May they preserve with each other sincere charity and peace and, if it be Thy Holy Will, grant that a Place of Thine abiding be established once again to be a Sanctuary and a Light. Through Jesus Christ our Lord. Amen.

From *The Coracle*

LEGENDS AND DREAMS

THE METROPOLIS OF DREAMS

There is another Iona than the Iona of sacred memories and prophecies; Iona the metropolis of dreams. None can understand it who does not see it through its pagan light, its Christian light, its singular blending of paganism and romance and spiritual beauty.

Fiona Macleod: Iona

THE ISLAND OF THE DRUIDS

I feel sure, despite the legends, that this was no case of Columba's just having happened to land here—as early European navigators happened to land on a West Indian island. Iona was an important centre in that early Druidic world. The usual scholar's or historian's talk about the savages and barbarians who inhabited the land in Columba's time is very misleading. In this respect the Christian ethic certainly pre-judged the Druidic truth. We do know, for example, that one king, Fergus, went to Iona for his coronation; and in that same isle he was buried, a generation before Columba landed. We learn, too, that the isle had a great number of standing stones, and late travellers talk of the existence of a Druidic temple of twelve stones, each with a human body buried beneath it. These wise early missionaries of Christianity did not believe in violence and destruction. They sprinkled the pagan monoliths with holy water and carved on them their Christian emblems. . . . In Scotland to this day we find great menhirs with a Cross on one side and the Pagan emblems on the other.

. . . Out of much undisciplined reading about that ancient pre-Christian world, what has always struck me is the extremely wide, if not universal, practice of what may be loosely called the standing-stone or Druidic religion. Even the attempt over many centuries to make of Europe one unified country of Catholic culture and religion, seems a small affair when set against the actual Druidic unification of that older world existing over a period of time so great that we hardly dare to compute it.

For example, the 360 *sculptured* stones of Iona make one traveller (C. F. Gordon Cumming) think of the Kaaba at Mecca. " The Kaaba at Mecca (which to all good Mahomedans is as sacred as was the Holy of Holies to the Israelites) had, from time immemorial, been accounted by all the people of Arabia, to be the very portal of Heaven. Until the time of Mahomet, it was surrounded by 360 *rude unsculptured monoliths*, which, to the degenerate Arabs, had become objects of actual worship, and in presence of which, they were wont to sacrifice red cocks to the sun (just as the people in these Western Isles have continued to do, almost to the present day, though of course in ignorance of the original meaning of this ancestral custom).

More unflinching than the Christian reformers of Iona, Mahomet would admit of no compromise. Like the Synod of Argyll, he resolved on the destruction of these " monuments of idolatrie," and so his iconoclastic followers did his bidding, and destroyed them utterly.

. . . That Columba and his brethren, who built their little church of wood and its surrounding cells of wattle and daub, so that now nothing remains of their habitation, should also have reared these 360 stones is manifestly absurd, even had we no collateral aids to judgment, such as the remarkable twelve-stone circle, with its radiating lines, at Callanish in Lewis.

Moreover, until quite recent times, Highlanders spoke of Iona as the " Druid's Isle," and long after Columba had landed on it, the Irish continued to call it by that name.

One further thing has struck me, too, in this matter, and that is the obvious feeling of respect that these early Christian missionaries had for the older faith. There was manifestly no bitter rancour, no outflowing of righteous wrath against a degenerate creed. As he made the cross on the monolith, so Columba in one of his written prayers calls Christ his Druid: " mo drui . . . mac Dé " (my Druid . . . son of God).

Neil M. Gunn: Off in a Boat

ST. BRIDE OF THE ISLES

Before ever Colum came across the Moyle to the island of Iona . . . there lived upon the south-east slope of Dun-I a poor herdsman named Dùvach. . . . He was a prince in his own land, though none on Ioua save the Arch-Druid knew what his name was. . . . In his youth he had been accused of having done a wrong against a noble maiden of the blood. When her child was born he was made to swear across her dead body that he would be true to the daughter for whom she had given up her life, that he would rear her in a holy place, but away from Eire, and that he would never set foot within that land again. . . . So it was that by advice of Aodh of the Druids . . . he took boat with some wayfarers bound for Alba. But in the Moyle a tempest arose, and the frail galley was driven northward, and at sunrise was cast . . . upon the south end of Ioua, that is now Iona. Only two lived; Dùghall Donn (Dùvach) and the little child. This was at the place where, on a day of days in a year that was not yet come, St. Colum landed in his coracle, and gave thanks on his bended knees.

When, warmed by the sun, they rose, they found themselves in a waste place. . . . The Arch-Druid of Iona approached, with his white-robed priests. A grave welcome was given to the stranger. While the youngest of the servants of God was entrusted with the child, the Arch-Druid took Dùghall aside and questioned him. It was not till the third day that the old man gave his decision. Dùghall Donn was to abide on Iona if he so willed: but the child was to stay. . . . A little land to till would be given him, and all that he might need. But of his past he was to say no word. . . . He was to be known simply as Dùvach. The child, too, was to be named Bride, for that was the way the same Brigit was called in the Erse of the Isles.

To the question of Dùghall, that was thenceforth Dùvach, as to why he laid so great stress on the child . . . Cathal the Arch-Druid replied thus: " My kinsman Aodh of the Golden Hair who sent you here was wiser than Hugh the King and all the Druids of Aoimag. Truly this child is an Immortal. There is an ancient prophecy concerning her. . . . There shall be, it says, a spotless maid born of a virgin of the ancient immemorial race in Innisfail. And when for the seventh time the sacred year has come, she will hold Eternity in her lap as a white flower. Her maiden breasts shall swell with milk for the Prince of the World. She shall give suck to the King of the Elements. So I say unto you, Dùvach, go in peace. Take unto thyself a wife, and live upon the place I will give thee on the east side of Iona. Treat Bride as though she were thy spirit, but leave her much alone, and let her learn of the sun and the wind. In the fulness of time the prophecy shall be fulfilled."

. . . Bride lived the hours of her days upon the slopes of Dun-I, herding the sheep, or in following the kye upon the green hillocks and grassy dunes of what then, as now, was called the Machar. The beauty of the world was her daily food. The spirit within her was like sunlight behind a white flower. The birdeens in the green bushes sang for joy when they saw her blue eyes. The tender prayers that were in her heart for all the beasts and birds, for helpless children, and tired women, and all who were old, were often seen flying above her head in the form of white doves of sunshine.

Fiona Macleod: The Sin-Eater and Other
Legendary Moralities

BRIDE ON DUN-I

Sting me not, nettle please!
God grant you perfect ease,
I would not grievance do
Unto your root or you.

Only awhile I'd spread
My hands beneath my head,
And here on grassy bank
Our souls' Creator thank.

Who gave to you and me
Light from His sacred Tree,
Who me and you did light
With superhuman sight.

So that we breathe within
Deeper than root of sin,
Drinking from Earth's green breast
Joy and eternal rest.

Lovely above my hair
Mid the blue vault of air
Lark in the height of Heaven
Sings to the planets seven.

Deeper and deeper yet,
Still God lets down his net
Till in earth's darkest ground
Beauty and light are found.

All that the earth doth yield,
Insect or flower of field,
In all these things He saw
Never a stain or flaw.

Never a hint of sin
Saw he without, within.
Lo! He made all things well,
Eyebright and asphodel.

Isobel Wylie Hutchison

DRUIDIC RITES ON DUN-I

The still weather had come, and all the isles lay in beauty.

. . . It was while the dew was yet wet on the grass that Bride came out of her father's house and went up the steep slope of Dun-I. The crying of the ewes and lambs at the pastures came plaintively against the dawn. The lowing of the kye arose from the sandy hollows by the shore, or from the meadows on the lower slopes. Through the whole island went a rapid trickling sound, most sweet to hear: the myriad voices of twittering birds, from the dotterel in the seaweed to the larks climbing the blue spirals of heaven.

. . . When at last, a brief while before sunrise, she reached the summit of the Scuir, that is so small a hill and yet seems so big in Iona where it is the sole peak, she found three young Druids there, ready to tend the sacred fire the moment the sun-rays should kindle it. Each was clad in a white robe, with fillets of oak leaves; and each had a golden armlet. They made a quiet obeisance as she approached. One stepped forward with a flush in his face because of her beauty, that was as a sea-wave for grace, and a flower for purity, and sunlight for joy, and moonlight for peace, and wind for fragrance.

" Thou mayst draw near if thou wilt, Bride, daughter of Dùvach," he said, with something of reverence as of grave courtesy in his voice: " for the holy Cathal hath said that the Breath of the Source of all is upon thee. It is not lawful for women to be here at this moment, but thou hast the law shining upon thy face and in thine eyes. Hast thou come to pray?"

But at that moment a low cry came from one of his companions. He turned, and re-joined his fellows. Then all three sank upon their knees, and with outstretched arms hailed the rising of God.

As the sun rose, a solemn chant swelled from their lips, ascending as incense through the silent air. The glory of the new day came soundlessly. Peace was in the blue heaven, on the blue-green sea, on the green land. There was no wind, even where the currents of the deep moved in shadowy purple. The sea itself was silent, making no more than a sighing slumber-breath round the white sands of the isle, or a hushed whisper where the tide lifted the long weed that clung to the rocks.

In what strange, mysterious way Bride did not see; but as the three Druids held their hands before the sacred fire there was a faint crackling, then three thin spirals of blue smoke rose, and soon dusky red and wan yellow tongues of flame moved to and fro. The sacrifice of God was made. Out of the immeasurable heaven He had come, in his golden chariot. Now, in the wonder and mystery of His love, he was re-born upon the world, re-born a little fugitive flame upon a low hill in a remote island. Great must be His love that He could die thus daily in a thousand places: so great His love that He could give up His own body to daily death, and suffer the holy flame that was in the embers He illumined to be lighted and revered and then scattered to the four quarters of the world.

Bride could bear no longer the mystery of this great love. It moved her to an ecstasy. What tenderness of divine love that could thus redeem the world daily: what long-suffering for all the evil and cruelty done hourly upon the weeping earth: what patience with the bitterness of the blind fates! The beauty of the worship of Be'al was upon her as a golden glory. Her heart leaped to a song that could not be sung. The inexhaustible love and pity in her soul chanted a hymn that was heard of no Druid or mortal anywhere, but was known of the white spirits of Life.

Bowing her head, so that the glad tears fell warm as thunder-rain upon her hands, she rose and moved away.

Fiona Macleod: The Sin-Eater and Other
Legendary Moralities.

THE SONG OF BRIDE

This poem (here abbreviated) is founded upon the Gaelic legend that St. Bride was transported by angels from the Hebrides to Bethlehem on the first Christmas Eve, to become *the foster-mother of Christ, and to wrap Him in her mantle (from which she gets the Gaelic title Brigdhe-nam-Brat, Bride of the Mantle, or Plaid).**

It is a starlight night, the first Christmas Eve. Bride is walking on the white sands at the North End of Iona. The night is calm, and in the water the light of the moon and stars dances and shifts, ringed in dark circles as if caught in a net. Bride is alone, singing to herself.

Bride (Singing):
> What a beautiful night!
> The new moon, steely blue,
> Peers like a paring of light
> The floating cloud-wrack through
> And arrests me with her calm
> Here by the shimmering waste,
> Spending on the waters her psalm
> Voiceless, chaste.

> Silent voice, I listen!
> Through the clouds' soft yeast
> Lo! Out of a window
> Opened in the east
> One great star is shining,
> In the polished sand
> Underfoot reflected
> From this northern land.

> Here I love to wander,
> On this watery shore
> Underfoot to ponder
> And pass the round moon o'er.
> I might be some angel
> Leaning from a star
> To watch the world swinging
> In her cloudy car.

* The mantle was traditionally woven by Bride herself on the island of Iona. It is nice to think of the infant Jesus being swaddled in a bit of Highland homespun!

Swinging, ever swinging
    On God's chain of thought,
Till Imagination
    Shall at last be brought
To work the will of Heaven
    In earth's heavy clay
And each atom dances
    On its starry way.
(She pauses)
    Heigho! I am rather tired!
I would like to sleep
Outside to-night, if it were not so cold,
Watching how the moonlight is rolled
Like a ball on the dark-blue deep
Heaving round shadows.

And so Bride came to the top of the beach
Beneath the sandhills, and sat down
    Out of the waves' reach.
    From foot to crown
She was wrapped in a mantle of dark blue cloth
(The colour of her eyes) spun by her own hands;
She wore no hood, and her gold hair was plaited in bands
    About her face, pale as a moth
    Flickering on a June night
Over the yellow Oenothera in some garden-place;
To the shimmering moonlight she lent grace,
And warmth to the remote and frosty stars.

     .   .   .   .

On the beach an oyster-catcher under the moon
In his handsome plumage of black and white
    With feet bright red and quaint,
Lingered quietly near, for it was his boon
To be her servant. A little timid he was, not quite
    At his ease beside a saint,
For he was only a bird
Who obeyed God's Word
    Unconsciously.

The two were alone in the starlight with the sea.
On the beach it sounded thunderously,
Bringing in a deep reverberant note
        Of laughter and joy,
And sometimes of a sudden it smote
        The rocks with a loud report
        Like the clapping of hands,
As if from its vast theatre it contemplated God's laws
        With delight and applause.
        Whitely in the starlight it shone,
And over Bride's head the heavens were tremulously drawn
        In numbered splendour.
She leaned her back in restful surrender
        Against a rock, and gazed
        At God's handiwork, constantly amazed
        By His loveliness and wonder.

.   .   .   .

        As Bride gazed she saw a falling star
        Struck from the wheels of Cassiopeia's car.
        Swiftly as thought it vanished in the tide,
        And lo! Two angels standing by her side!

        With open hands
        They waited by her on the glimmering sands,
        Clad in a brightness far beyond the reach
        Of human speech.
More dazzling than the light of frost
On snowy Alpine fields by sunlight crost.
" Brigdhe!"—they said, " Fear not at all,
To-night in Bethlehem is born
The Son of Man, and ere the morn
Thy mantle blue shall be his shawl."

Bride laughed and clapped her hands for joy
At thought of the little boy
        (Long promised)
Who was to help everyone.

70

And now she understood why a new sun
Had appeared in the east overhead.
Her body felt heavy as lead
To her soaring mind,
Dazzled and half-blind
          She swayed,
But the angels caught her and wrapped her in her plaid
          And she was lifted
          In their arms.

          Far below there shifted
          The blue Atlantic seas
          Shouting glad alarums
          Round the Hebrides.
          Now with wings outspread
          Through the starry sky
          The angels fly,
          One bearing Bride's feet,
          The other pillowing her head,
          Fast asleep—smiling.
Forgotten forever Iona, forgotten the white sands,
Forgotten the summer flowers of the Hebridean machair-
          lands
          So numerous, so beguiling,
In the new engrossing vision she has seen
          Of a little shepherd-boy
          Piping on the daisied green
          Full of joy;
Of a little sunburnt fisher-lad
          Half-clad,
Clambering into boats,
Dabbling his kilted coats
          On Galilee,
Of a little Carpenter full of glee
Chipping boats for His mother to see.
          She is gone with the speed of light,
          And the night
          Falls deeper on the Highlands.

Over the islands
A wind rises, and soft white clouds
Floating, cover the stars
In ragged streamers and bars.
She is gone.
Forgotten forever her lad,
The oyster-catcher,
The servant of Bride,
Who knows that none can match her.

Left alone
By the dark incoming tide
For a little while he seeks to fly
After her, then with despairing cry,
Indignant, down he drops again
To the shore below
And runs distressfully to and fro
Complaining bitterly
Of the Saint's treatment of her faithful lad,
Sulky and very sad,
Calling his own name and hers forever more
About the lonely shore.
" Gille-gille-gille-gille-B-r-i-d-e !
Gille-gille-gille-gille-B-r-i-d-e !"

Isobel Wylie Hutchison

THE FESTIVAL OF THE BIRDS

At dawn . . . Colum, sitting upon the strewed fern
that was his bed, rubbed his eyes that were heavy with
weariness and fasting and long prayer. . . . On the ledge
of the hole that was in the eastern wall of his cell he saw a
bird. He leaned his elbow upon the *leabhar-aifrionn** that
was by his side. Then he spoke.

" Is there song upon thee, O *Bru-dhearg*?"†

Then the Red-breast sang, and the singing was so
sweet that tears came into the eyes of Colum, and he thought
the sunlight that was streaming from the east was melted
into that lilting sweet song. It was a hymn that the
Bru-dhearg sang, and it was thus:—

* Missal.   † (literally) Red-breast.

72

Holy, holy, holy,
    Christ upon the Cross;
My little nest was here,
    Hidden in the moss.

Holy, holy, holy,
    Christ was pale and wan,
His eyes beheld me singing,
    Bron, bron, mo bron.

Holy, holy, holy,
    Come near, O wee brown bird,
Christ spake: and lo, I lighted
    Upon the Living Word.

Holy, holy, holy,
    I heard the mocking scorn!
But *holy, holy, holy*,
    I sang against the thorn!

Holy, holy, holy,
    Ah, His brow was bloody:
Holy, holy, holy,
    All my breast was ruddy.

Holy, holy, holy,
    " Christ's bird shalt thou be!"
This said Mary Virgin,
    There on Calvary.

Holy, holy, holy,
    A wee brown bird am I;
But my breast is ruddy
    For I saw Christ die.

Holy, holy, holy,
    By this ruddy feather,
Colum, call thy monks and
    All the birds together.

And at that Colum rose. Awe was upon him, and joy.
He went out and told all to the monks. Then he said
Mass out on the green sward. The yellow sunshine was
warm upon his grey hair. The love of God was warm in
his heart.

" Come, all ye birds!" he cried.

And lo, all the birds of the air flew nigh. The golden
eagle soared from the Cuchullins in far-off Skye, and the
osprey from the wild lochs of Mull; the gannet from above
the clouds, and the fulmar and petrel from the green wave:
the cormorant and the skua from the weedy rock, and the
plover and the kestrel from the machar: the corbie and the
raven from the moor, and the snipe and the bittern and the
heron: the cuckoo and the cushat from the woodland: the
crane from the swamp, the lark from the sky, and the mavis
and the merle from the green bushes: the yellow-yite, the
shilfa, and the lintie, the gyalvonn and the wren and the
redbreast, one and all, every creature of the wings, they
came at the bidding.

" Peace ! " cried Colum.

" Peace!" cried all the Birds, and even the Eagle, the
Kestrel, the Corbie, and the Raven cried *Peace, Peace!*

" I will say the Mass," said Colum the White.

And with that he said the Mass. And he blessed the
birds.

When the last chant was sung, only the Bru-dhearg
remained.

Fiona Macleod: The Three Marvels of Iona

COLUMBA AND THE FLOUNDER

Columba was one day in the strand of the small-fry
and he trampled on a beautiful little fair Flounder and hurt
her tail. The poor little Flounder cried out as loud as she
could—

Thou Colum big and clumsy,
With the crooked crosswise feet,
Much didst thou to me of injust
When thou didst trample on my tail.

74

Columba was angry at being taunted with having crooked feet and he said—
> If I am crooked-footed,
> Be thou wry-mouthed.

And he left her that way.

Alexander Carmichael: Carmina Gadelica

THE LEGEND OF ST. ORAN

Both in the oral legend and in that early monkish chronicle alluded to, Columba is represented as either suggesting or accepting immolation of a living victim as a sacrifice to consecrate the church he intended to build.

One story is that he received a divine intimation to the effect that a monk of his company must be buried alive, and that Odran offered himself. In the earliest known rendering " Colum Cille said to his people: ' It is well for us that our roots should go underground here,' and he said to them, ' It is permitted to you that some one of you go under the earth of this island to consecrate it.' Odran rose up readily, and thus he said: ' If thou wouldst accept me, I am ready for that.' . . . Odran then went to heaven. Colum Cille then founded the Church of Hi."

. . . The legend, which has crystallised into a popular saying, " Uir, ùir, air sùil Odhrain! mu'n labhair e tuille comhraidh "—" Earth, earth on Oran's eyes, lest he further blab "—avers that three days after the monk Oran or Odran was entombed alive . . . Colum opened the grave to look once more on the face of the dead brother, when to the amazed fear of the monks and the bitter anger of the abbot himself, Oran opened his eyes and exclaimed, " There is no such great wonder in death, nor is hell what it has been described." . . . At this, Colum straightway cried the now famous Gaelic words, and then covered up poor Oran again.

. . . It would be a dark stain on Columba's character if this legend was true. But apart from the fact that

75

Adamnan does not speak of it or of Oran, the probabilities are against its truth. On the other hand, it is, perhaps, quite as improbable that there was no basis for the legend. I imagine the likelier basis to be that a Druid suffered death in this fashion under that earlier Odran of whom there is mention in the *Annals of the Four Masters:* possibly that Odhran himself was the martyr, and the Arch-Druid the person who had the " divine intimation." Again, before it be attributed to Columba, one would have to find if there is record of such an act having been performed among the Irish of that day. We have no record of it. It is not improbable that the whole legend is a symbolical survival, an ancient teaching of some elementary mystery through some real or apparent sacrificial rite.

Fiona Macleod: Iona

COLUMBA'S BAN ON WOMEN

Eilean Nam Ban (The Island of the Women) lies close to the Mull shore, just opposite the Abbey. To this place, according to tradition, Columba banished all women* and cows from Iona for a reason preserved in the old distich:—

Far am bi bo bidh bean,
S' far am bi bean bidh mallachadh.

Where there is a cow,
There will be a woman;
And where there is a woman,
There will be mischief.

* Probably the island was set apart for the wives of the labourers employed by the monks.

That the Saint's objection to women (if the tradition is well-founded) is limited to their presence in or near a monastic settlement is made clear by certain incidents in his life chronicled by Adamnan, *e.g.,* his concern for his kinswoman in the throes of a painful childbirth.

A DRUIDIC RITE

This is one of the many instances where a Druidic rite has received a Christian sanction.

Michael nam Buadh, Michael the Victorious, the conqueror of the powers of darkness, is the patron saint of the sea and maritime lands, of boats and boatmen, of horses and horsemen. His name is found all over the Celtic fringes of Britain, from Mount St. Michael in Cornwall to Ard Micheal, a name borne by two promontories, one in North and one in South Uist.

St. Michael is usually represented riding a milk-white steed, a three-pronged spear in his right hand and a three-cornered shield in his left.

On the Western seaboard and in the Hebrides, Michaelmas was in former times the great festival of the year. Although ostensibly a Christian festival, many of the rites associated with it are definitely of pagan origin, and were in all probability taken over from the ancient Samhuinn (Hallowe'en) festival.

" It is a day," says Dr. Carmichael, " when pagan cult and Christian doctrine meet and mingle like lights and shadows on their own Highland hills."

St. Michael being the patron saint of horses, horse-racing was a prominent part of the celebration. The eighteenth century traveller, Pennant, was told by Bishop Pococke that on the eve of St. Michael's Day the islanders of Iona brought all their horses to a small green hill on which stood a cairn surrounded by a circle of stones. " Round this hill they all made the turn sunwise, thus unwittingly dedicating their horses to the sun."

F. Marian McNeill

ST. MICHAEL AND ST. COLUMBA

On Iona there is, so far as I remember, no special spot sacred to St. Micheil*: but there is a legend that on the night Columba died Micheil came over the waves in a

---

* Apparently the writer was unaware of the Michaelmas cavalcade of which Bishop Pococke speaks.

rippling flood of light, which was a cloud of angelic wings, and that he sang a hymn to the soul of the saint before it took flight for its heavenly fatherland. No one heard that hymn save Colum, but I think that he who first spoke of it remembered a more ancient legend of how Manannan came to Cuchullin when he was in the country of the Shee, when Liban laughed.

Fiona Macleod: Iona

AN OFFERING TO THE SEA

On Maundy Thursday, the people living on the Western seaboard and in the Isles used to make offerings of mead, ale or gruel to the sea, in the belief that by sending the fruit of the land to the sea, the fruit of the sea—seaweed to be used as manure—would come to the land. This custom was originally carried out on one of the old Celtic Quarter Days. In Iona, Maundy Thursday was long known as *Diardaoin a Brochain Mhoir*, Great Gruel Thursday. The ceremony has been described by Dr. Carmichael:—

" As the day merged from Wednesday to Thursday, a man walked to the waist into the sea and poured out whatever offering had been prepared, chanting:

O God of the Sea,
Put weed in the drawing wave
To enrich the ground,
To shower on us food.

Those behind the offerer took up the chant and wafted it along the sea-shore, on the midnight air, the darkness of night and the rolling of the waves made the scene weird and impressive. In 1860 the writer conversed in Iona with a middle-aged man whose father, when young, had taken part in this ceremony."

In Lewis the custom was carried on into the nineteenth century, and so strong was the belief in the potency of the rite to procure a plentiful crop that it took the ministers several years to persuade the natives to abandon " this ridiculous bit of superstition." Martin gives us a description of the rite as preserved in that island:—

" The inhabitants of Bragar had an ancient custom of sacrifice to a sea-god called Shony,* at Hallowtide in the manner of the following: the inhabitants of the island came to the church of St. Malvay, having each man his provision along with him; every family furnished a peck of malt, and this was brewed into ale; one of their number was picked out to wade into the sea up to the middle, and carrying a cup of ale in his hand, standing still in that posture, cried with a loud voice, saying, ' Shony, I give you this cup of ale, hoping you will be so kind as to send us plenty of sea-ware for enriching the ground for the ensuing year,' and so threw the cup of ale into the sea. This was performed in the night time. At his return to land they all went to church, where there was a candle burning upon the altar; and then, standing silent for a little time, one of them gave a signal at which the candle was put out, and immediately all of them went to the fields, where they fell a-drinking their ale, and spent the remainder of the night in dancing and singing."

F. Marian McNeill

SHANNY TICKLE-MY-TOES

My Hebridean nurse had often told me of Shony, a mysterious sea-god, and I know I spent much time in wasted adoration.

. . . I was amused not long ago to hear a little girl singing, as she ran wading through the foam of a troubled sunlit sea, as it broke on those wonderful white sands of Iona:—

" Shanny, Shanny, Shanny,
Catch my feet and tickle my toes!
And if you can, Shanny, Shanny, Shanny,
I'll go with you where no one knows!"

I have no doubt this daintier Shanny was my old friend Shony, whose more terrifying way was to clutch boats by

* Dr. George Henderson suggests that Shony may be identified with Sjofn, one of the goddesses in the *Edda*.

the keel and drown the sailors, and make a death-necklace of their teeth. An evil Shony: for once he netted a young girl who was swimming in a loch, and when she would not give him her love he tied her to a rock, and to this day her long brown hair may be seen floating in the shallow green wave at the ebb of the tide. One need not name the place!

Fiona Macleod: Iona

THE STONE OF DESTINY

Near St. Columba's Tomb there stood formerly one of the most ancient and sacred of Iona's relics—the Black Stones of Iona, so called not from their colour, but from the black doom that fell on any who dared to violate an oath sworn upon them. . . .

There is a tradition that the Coronation Stone in Westminster Abbey was originally one of the famous Black Stones. Its legendary history is very old, for it is believed to have been reverenced as Jacob's pillow by the tribes who brought it from the East in the first wave of Celtic emigration. " On this stone—the old Druidic Stone of Destiny, sacred among the Gael before Christ was born—Columba crowned Aidan King of Argyll. Later the stone was taken to Dunstaffnage, where the Lords of the Isles were made princes: thence to Scone, where the last of the Celtic kings of Scotland was crowned on it. It now lies in Westminster Abbey, a part of the Coronation Chair, and since Edward I every British monarch has been crowned upon it. If ever the Stone of Destiny be moved again, that writing on the wall will be the signature of a falling dynasty."

Fiona Macleod

Skene questions all its history before its use for Scottish coronations at Scone.

Sir Archibald Geikie has pronounced the stone to be like similar stones plentiful in Argyll and Fife. But stones, as some one comments, are very similar the world over, and if like any other stone, why choose it for reverence?

IMPRESSIONS AND TRIBUTES

DR. JOHNSON AND BOSWELL

19th October, 1773

After a tedious sail, which, by our following various turnings of the coast of Mull, was extended to about forty miles, it gave us no small pleasure to perceive a light in the village at Icolmkill, in which almost all the inhabitants of the island live, close to where the ancient building stood. As we approached the shore, the tower of the cathedral, just discernible in the air, was a picturesque object.

When we had landed upon the sacred place, which, as long as I can remember, I had thought on with veneration, Dr. Johnson and I cordially embraced. We had long talked of visiting Icolmkill; and from the lateness of the season, were at times very doubtful whether we should be able to effect our purpose. To have seen it, even alone, would have given me great satisfaction; but the venerable scene was rendered much more pleasing by the company of my great and pious friend, who was no less affected by it than I was; and who has described the impressions it should make on the mind, with such strength of thought and energy of language, that I shall quote his words, as conveying my own sensations much more forcibly than I am capable of doing:

" We were now treading that illustrious Island, which was once the luminary of the Caledonian regions, whence savage clans and roving barbarians derived the benefits of knowledge, and the blessings of religion. To abstract the mind from all local emotion would be impossible, if it were endeavoured, and would be foolish if it were possible. Whatever withdraws us from the power of our senses, whatever makes the past, the distant, or the future, predominate over the present, advances us in the dignity of thinking beings. Far from me, and from my friends, be such frigid philosophy as may conduct us indifferent and unmoved over any ground which has been dignified by wisdom, bravery, or virtue. That man is little to be envied, whose patriotism would not gain force upon the plain of Marathon, or whose piety would not grow warmer among the ruins of *Iona.*"

Upon hearing that Sir Allan MacLean was arrived, the inhabitants, who still consider themselves as the people of MacLean, to whom the island formerly belonged, though the Duke of Argyll has at present possession of it, ran eagerly to him.

We were accommodated that night in a large barn, the island affording no lodging that we should have liked so well. Some good hay was strewed at one end of it, to form a bed for us, upon which we lay with our clothes on; and we were furnished with blankets from the village. Each of us had a portmanteau for a pillow. When I wakened in the morning, and looked round me, I could not help smiling at the idea of the chief of the Macleans, the great English moralist, and myself, lying thus extended in such a situation.

James Boswell: Journal of a Tour to the
Hebrides with Samuel Johnson, LL.D.

SIR WALTER SCOTT
(*From a Letter to George Ellis*)

July 29, 1810

My dear Ellis,—I am just returning from a delightful Highland tour in which we have scarcely encountered a shower of rain. . . . We entered the sound of Ulva with pipes playing and banners displayed, and were received by

Staffa's people, who were all under arms, with a discharge of artillery. The next day we were escorted to Staffa and Iona. The cavern well deserves its renown. . . . I penetrated over the broken columns to the very extremity but some of our party took fright. The Hebridean boatmen who are great admirers of poetry and music and still hold the character of the Vates in ancient respect did me the honour to christen a stone at the mouth of the cavern by the sounding title of *Clachan an Bhaird Sassenach More* or the Stone of the great Saxon poet. One of them made a long oration on the subject with much gesture and emphasis, but I was obliged to take the contents as he did my poetical talents, upon trust. Only, I learned, he praised me for " burnishing the armour of the mighty dead " and for being the friend of the chieftain Staffa. Iona is a very singular place—the remains of the Church though not beautiful are very curious and nothing can be more wonderful than to see the numbers of sculptured monuments of priests and warriors in a place so extremely desolate and miserable. The inhabitants are in the last state of poverty and wretchedness. Fisheries might relieve them, but I see no other resource, for the island though fertile, considering all things, does not produce food for the inhabitants, and they have neither money nor commodities to induce importation of provisions. We did not stay so long as I could have wished, being threatened with a gale of wind—no pleasant prospect in an open boat on the Atlantic.

(From a Letter to Joanna Baillie)
Ulva House, July 19, 1810

I had become a sort of favourite with the Hebridean boatmen I suppose from my anxiety about their old customs and they were much pleased to see me get over the obstacles which stopped some of the party. So they took the whim of christening a great stone seat at the mouth of the cavern Clachan-an-Bairdh or the Poet's Stone. It was consecrated with a pibroch which the echoes rendered tremendous and a glass of whisky not poured forth in the ancient mode of libation but turned over the throats of the Assistants. . . .

83

When the fun was over (in which, strange as it may seem, the men were quite serious) we went to Iona where there are some ancient and curious monuments. From this rude and remote island the light of Christianity shone forth on Scotland and Ireland. The ruins are of a rude architecture but curious to the Antiquary. Our return hither was less comfortable; we had to row twenty miles against an Atlantic tide and some wind besides the pleasure of seeing occasional squalls gathering to windward. The ladies were sick especially poor Hannah Mackenzie and none of the gentlemen escaped except Staffa and myself. The men however cheered by the pipes and by their own interesting boat songs which are uncommonly wild and beautiful, one man leading and the others answering in chorus, kept pulling away without apparently the least sign of fatigue and we reached Ulva at ten at night tolerably wet and well disposed for bed.

KEATS ON IONA

(From a letter to his brother, Thomas Keats, in London)

" July 26th (1818).—Well—we had a most wretched walk of 37 miles across the island of Mull and then we cross'd to Iona or Icolmkill. . . . I know not whether you have heard much about this Island, I never did before I came nigh it. It is rich in the most interesting Antiquities. Who would expect to find the ruins of a fine cathedral, of Cloisters, Colleges, Monasteries and Nunneries in so remote an Island? The beginning of these things was in the sixth Century under the superstition of a would-be Bishop-saint who landed from Ireland and chose the spot from its Beauty—for at that time the now treeless place was covered with magnificent Woods. Columba in the Gaelic is Colum, signifying Dove—Kill signifies Church and I is as good as Island—so Icolmkill means the Island of Saint Columba's Church. Now this Saint became the Dominic of the barbarian Christians of the north and was famed also far south—but more especially was reverenced by the Scots the Picts the Norwegians the Irish. In the course of years the

I(s)land was considered the most holy ground of the north, and the old Kings of the afore-mentioned nations chose it for their burial-place. We were shown a spot in the Churchyard where they say 61 Kings are buried 48 Scotch from Fergus 2nd to Mackbeth 8 Irish 4 Norwegian and 1 french—they lie in rows compact. Then we were shown other matters of interest of later date but still very ancient— many tombs of Highland Chieftains—their effigies in complete armour face upwards—black and moss covered— Abbots and Bishops of the island always of one of the chief Clans. There were plenty Macleans and Macdonnels, among these latter the famous Macdonel Lord of the Isles— There have been 300 crosses in the island but the Presbyterians destroyed all but two, one of which is a very fine one and completely covered with a shaggy coarse moss. The old Schoolmaster is an ignorant little man but reckoned very clever, showed us these things—He is a Macklean and as much above 4 foot as he is under 4 foot 3 inches—he stops at one glass of wiskey unless you press another and at the second unless you press a third."

(*He then goes on to describe Staffa, which, unlike Iona, inspired a poem.*)

From *Keats's* Letters, edited by Maurice Buxton Forman

MENDELSSOHN
Glasgow, August 10, 1829

Iona, one of the Hebrides-sisters—there is truly a very Ossianic and sweetly sad sound about that name—when in some future time I shall sit in a madly crowded assembly with music and dancing round me, and the wish arises to retire into the loneliest loneliness, I shall think of Iona, with its ruins of a once magnificent cathedral, the remains of a convent, the graves of ancient Scottish Kings and still more ancient northern pirate-princes—with their ships rudely carved on many a monumental stone. If I had my home on Iona, and lived there upon melancholy as other people do upon their rents, my darkest moment would be when in that wide space, that deals in nothing but cliffs and sea-gulls, suddenly a curl of steam should appear, followed by a ship and finally by a gay party in veils and frock-coats, which would look for an hour at the ruins and graves and the three little huts for the living, and then move off again. This highly unjustifiable joke, occurring twice a week, and being almost the only thing to make one aware that there are such things as time and clocks in the world, would be as if the inhabitants of these old graves haunted the place in a ludicrous disguise. Opposite Iona stands a rocky island which, to complete the effect, looks like a ruined city.

Felix Mendelssohn: From Sebastian Hensels's
The Mendelssohn Family

It is said that this was the manner in which the overture, *The Hebrides*, took its rise: Mendelssohn's sisters asked him to tell them something about the Hebrides. " It cannot be told, only played," he said. No sooner spoken than he seated himself at the piano and played the theme which afterwards grew into the overture.

W. A. Lampadius: Life of Felix Mendelssohn

HIGHLAND DESTITUTION IN THE FORTIES

In 1846 *and following years, the failure of the potato crop deprived the people of the West Highlands of their staple article of diet and brought untold misery to the Highlands and Islands. Iona suffered with other districts and some indication of this suffering is given in the following passage from a report of the Destitution Committee of the Free Church in* 1847.

Nowhere did this section see more evident and manifest tokens of real want than in the Island of Iona, and on the opposite coast of the Island of Mull, in the district of Ross. They exceedingly regretted that they were unable to visit the whole of that district. The countenances of many of the people rendered any further inquiry unnecessary. The visiting members remarked here, as elsewhere, what, though apparently or comparatively trivial, is serious to the poor—their pigs and poultry gone. The former, without their wonted food, having literally disappeared in

Mull, Tyree, Ulva, and Iona; and in the part of the Ross of Mull they visited, two or three animals of this species were all they saw; and as for the latter species of property and profit to the humble cottager, the people of Iona told them, that being without feeding at home, their poultry wandered, and that eagles, ravens, and carrion crows fell upon them and devoured them. In Iona and the Ross of Mull, they found more sickness prevailing than elsewhere—fever, dysentery, and a particular type of typhus fever. The Committee grieve to state, that this has been confirmed by subsequent accounts. Mr. Donald Maclean, merchant, Bunessan, writes thus to the Secretary, January 13th:— " There are several families in this district actually in a dying state from starvation and sickness. Families consisting of from six to nine children, besides parents, are days without anything to eat except shell-fish and sea-ware, except when relieved by a handful of meal from those who have some; and what I have stated is little of what I have witnessed in visiting some of the families. I sincerely trust, whatever supplies the Committee may send to this place may be sent as speedily as can be by any means. The sickness is so great, with other calamities, that the number of deaths some days are between Ross and Iona from two to five. I am sorry to add, that sickness is still on the increase, particularly British cholera and dysentery."

QUEEN VICTORIA ANCHORS OFF IONA

Prince Albert, the Prince of Leinengen, the Duke of Norfolk, Earl Grey and Sir James Clark landed on the island in August, 1847, while the Queen herself was contiguous on the royal yacht, at the time of the progress northward to Ardverikie; and they had a reception from the people as primitive and decorous as was probably given anywhere to any ancient Lord of the Isles. A few plainly dressed islanders stood on the shore, carrying tufted willow-wands, and prepared to act as an escort; the body of the people, for the most part decently dressed, stood behind, looking eagerly on as spectators, yet all maintaining a respectful distance; only a few children, in the usual fashion of the island, offered pebbles and shells for sale; and when the august visitors, after quietly surveying the curiosities of the place, returned to the barge, all the population gave loud voice in a hearty farewell cheer.

From *The Imperial Gazetteer*, edited by Rev. J. M. Wilson

ROBERT LOUIS STEVENSON

While a student at Edinburgh University, Robert Louis Stevenson spent three weeks in the tidal islet of Erraid, which lies off the Ross of Mull, and just over the Sound from Iona. The relief men for the Dhu Heartach lighthouse are stationed here. David Balfour, the hero of " Kidnapped," is wrecked on its shore at the beginning of his adventurous journey across country.

In a letter to his mother, Louis describes his journey from Oban to Iona, en route for Erraid, and his encounters with an entertaining artist, a charming girl, and a tough fowl.

Erraid, Thursday, August 5th, 1870

Hitherto I had enjoyed myself immensely, but to-day has been the crown. In the morning I met (Sam) Bough on board, with whom I am both surprised and delighted. He and I have read the same books, and discuss Chaucer, Shakespere, Marlowe, Fletcher and all the old authors. He can quote verses by the page, and has really a very pretty literary taste. Altogether, with all his roughness and buffonery, a more pleasant clever fellow you may seldom see. . . . To continue, after a little go in with Samuel, he going up on the bridge, I looked about to see who was there, and mine eye lighted on two girls, one of whom was sweet and pretty, talking to an old gentleman. " Eh bien," says I to myself, " that seems the best investment on board." So I sidled up to the old gentleman, got into conversation with him and so with the damsel; and thereupon, having used the patriarch as a ladder I kicked him down behind me. Who should my damsel prove but Amy Sinclair, daughter of Sir Tollemache. She certainly was the simplest, most naive specimen of girlhood ever I saw. By getting brandy and biscuit and generally coaching up her cousin, who was sick, I ingratiated myself; and so kept her the whole way to Iona, taking her into the cave at Staffa and generally making myself as gallant as possible. I was never so much pleased with anything in my life as her amusing absence of *mauvaise honte*: she was so sorry I wasn't going on to Oban again: didn't know how she could have enjoyed herself if I hadn't been there, and was so sorry we hadn't met on the Crinan. When we came back from Staffa, she and her aunt went down to have lunch; and a minute later up comes Miss Amy to ask me if I wouldn't think better of it and take some lunch with them. I couldn't resist that, so down I went; and there she displayed the full extent of her innocence. I must be sure to come to Thurso Castle the next time I was in Caithness and Upper Norwood (whence she would take me all over the Crystal Palace) when I was near London; and (most complete of all) she offered to call on us in Edinburgh. Wasn't it delicious?—she is a girl of sixteen or seventeen. . . . I never yet saw a girl so innocent and fresh, so perfectly modest without the least trace of prudery.

. . . The last stage of the steamer now approached, Miss Amy and I lamenting pathetically that Iona was so near. " People meet in this way," quoth she, " and then lose sight of one another so soon." We all landed together, Bough and I and the Rosses with their baggage; and went together over the ruins.

. . . The steamer left, and Miss Amy and her cousin waved their handkerchiefs until my arm in answering them was nearly broken. . . . Altogether, however, I was left in a pleasant state of mind. . . .

(*Louis and Sam are invited to dine with a party including, besides some of their fellow passengers, John Stuart Blackie, who was staying on the island.*)

But we had already committed ourselves by mistake to the wrong hotel, and, besides, we wished to be off as soon as wind and tide were against us to Erraid. At five, down we go to the Argyll Hotel and wait for dinner. Broth—" nice broth "—fresh herrings and a fowl had been promised. At 5.50, I get the shovel and tongs and drum them at the stairhead till a response comes from below that the nice broth is at hand. . . . At last in comes the tureen and the hand-maid lifts the cover. " Rice soup!" I yell; " O no! none o' that for me!——" " Yes," says Bough, savagely; " but Miss Amy didn't take *me* downstairs to eat salmon." Accordingly he is helped. How his face fell! . . . It was, purely and simply, rice and water. After this, we have another weary pause, and then herrings in a state of mash and potatoes like iron. " Send the potatoes out to Prussia for grape shot," was the suggestion. I dined off broken herring and dry bread. At last the supreme moment comes, and the fowl in a lordly dish is carried in. On the cover being raised, there is something so forlorn and miserable about the aspect of the animal that we both roar with laughter. . . . However to work Bough falls until the sweat stands on his brow and a dismembered leg falls, dull and leaden like, on to my dish. To eat it was simply impossible. . . . Nothing for it now but to order boat and bill. " That fowl," says Bough to the landlady, " is of a breed I know. I knew the cut of its jib whenever it was put down. That was the grandmother of the cock that frightened Peter." . . . " Na-na, it's no' so old," says the landlady, " but it eats hard." . . . With more raillery we pay six shillings for our festival and run over to Erraid, shaking the dust of the Argyll Hotel from off our feet.*

Robert Louis Stevenson: Letters, Vol. I

A DISTINGUISHED GEOLOGIST

I once spent a delightful week in Iona, where a comfortable inn serves as excellent headquarters for the stay. There was a copy there of Reeve's edition of Adamnan's *Life of St. Columba.* Reading the volume where it was written, and amidst the very localities which it describes, and where the saint lived and died, one gets so thoroughly into the spirit of the place, the present seems to fade so far away, and the past to shine out again so clearly, that as one traces the faint lines of the old monastic enclosure, the

* Needless to say, the Argyll Hotel is a very different place nowadays.

mill-stream and the tracks which the monks must have followed in their errands over the island, one would hardly be surprised to meet the famous white horse and even the gentle Columba himself. But apart from its overpowering historic interest, Iona has the charm of most exquisite beauty and variety in its topography. Its western coast, rugged and irregular, has been cut into bays, clefts and headlands by the full surge of the open Atlantic. Its eastern side is flanked by the broad, smooth, calm Sound, which, where it catches the reflection of a cloudless sky, rivals the Mediterranean in the depths of its blue; while towards the north, where the water shallows over acres of white shell-sand it glistens with the green of an emerald. Then, as if to form a fitting background to this blaze of colour, the granite of the opposite shores of Mull glows with a warm pink hue as if it were ever catching the reflection of a gorgeous sunset. For wealth and variety of tints, I know of no spot of the same size to equal this isle of the saints.

Sir Archibald Geikie: Scottish Reminiscences

A PARTY OF MUSICIANS

When a man gives out much, he must absorb much; and it is good to live with the gods for a bit; that is why some folk made pilgrimage to the Western Isles of Scotland. It is quite possible to miss the gods there too, if you go by tourist steamer and allow yourself to be dumped on the island of Iona in a small boat with other passengers, shown the burial ground of the Kings of Scotland, conducted round the Cathedral . . . and shepherded back to the steamer once more.

. . . To win Iona's secret you must make it your home for a time; mix with the people; help them to gather in their hay; wander for long stretches on the cliffs round the coast, with the cries of innumerable sea-birds in your ears; lie on your back in the crystal-clear water looking up into the limitless blue; and in late evening, when all is quiet, walk in the very pathway of St. Columba. It is then that Iona becomes " Land of Heart's Desire, Isle of Youth."

If Iona is the Isle of Saints, Eigg is the Island of Heroes. Translated into music, Iona is Debussy, Eigg is Wagner. Eigg lies well to the north of Iona, and is just so much more rugged and dramatic in its conformation.

Speaking generally, the eastern side of the Hebridean islands is stern reality; the western side, romance.

Out to sea is the Island of Rum, with its giant sugar-loaf peaks, behind which the sun sets, and leaves them indescribably soft and purple. To the north are the Coolins of Skye looking like vast cathedrals, and all forming a great stage on which the gods themselves might appear without causing any surprise. Here is the land of giant stepping-stones, singing sands, magic wells and fairy pools. Here, too, are queen-like women, with eyes grown regal with looking on nature's palaces.

To all this came a company of fifteen friends [in the summer of 1913] to be initiated into its magic by Kenneth Macleod, the poet-priest who helped Marjory Kennedy-Fraser so much in the quest for Hebridean songs.

[*The party, which included Tobias Matthay and his gifted wife; Marjory Kennedy-Fraser, his sister-in-law; and Myra Hess, his most distinguished pupil, made its head-quarters in Eigg*]. . . . Old songs were revived, old tales were re-told, old dances that seemed like the dances of cave-men were performed in the barn in the evenings. Everyone was fey, and seemed to assume the spirit of faraway ancestors. . . . It seemed the time for which Walt Whitman must have written his Mystic Trumpeter, for the words rang out with a peculiar significance:—

Hark! Some wild trumpeter—some strange musician
Hovering unseen in air, vibrates capricious thoughts
    to-night. . . .
Blow, trumpeter, free and clear—I follow thee. . . .
Thy song expands my numb'd, imbonded spirit, thou
    freest, launchest me,
Floating and basking upon Heaven's lake.

. . . All too soon this time of enchantment had to come to an end, bundles had to be re-strapped, the petty details of life remembered, and the steamer boarded on the eastern side of the island—the side of stern reality..

Jessie Henderson Matthay: Life of Tobias Matthay

A HIGHLAND NOVELIST

A steady small rain was carried against us, and up the Sound with it came a considerable swell. Though the weather looked anything but promising, the glass was steady at nearly 30. Very reluctantly the Mate took down his precious sail, and we entered the Sound of Iona.

We had intended anchoring in the Bull Hole . . . but now, as we passed it on the north side and saw it hemmed in between gaunt granite rocks, it looked dull and anything but inviting. . . . I suddenly made up my mind to land at Port-na-Fraing. It was not shown on our chart, but we headed for the house and discovered the anchorage just a little south of it. A short reef of black rocks half guards its southern side, and the slipway of wet sand looks smooth as cement. The Mate, standing over the bow, could tell the depth of water at a glance, for the bottom was white sand and brown weed. He signalled me inside the outmost point of rock, just clear of the tide race. I could almost find time to be amused at his easy air of assurance.

But the engine, going slow, showed an entirely new belief in discipline. She accepted neutral, went ahead again, reversed, and remained running while the anchor was let go. It all seemed like a fairy story, and with proper solemnity we attribute it to some miraculous influence from the Island. The Crew took the depth—a couple of fathoms, with about two hours of ebb to run. Perfect—with good holding in tough weed. The heavens acknowledged our gratitude, drew the mists about us, opened their gates, and let the rain descend solidly. We had reached Iona.

In oilskins and long boots, the Crew and I got ashore at the sandy slip, and using a half-broken oar as a roller, pulled up the dinghy clear of the surf. The sand, composed of the pulverised shells of land snails, was so fine that it stuck to our hands and coated the rope. In striking

93

contrast to the Mull shore opposite, where the broken-down granite remains sharp-edged, here the pebbles were smooth and rounded and beautifuly and variously coloured. There was immediately the feeling of landing on a different, almost a strange and foreign, shore, though it was yet more intimate, as a shore of tradition, or dream, or actual past experience is intimate. On the right hand the conjunction was seen in a massive rugged boulder of red granite lying on the smooth greenish-blue water-worn rock. At the head of the little slipway, where two row boats were drawn up, springs of water came through the clean pebbles, and the scent of clover was in the air. Masses of ragged robin gave way to eyebright and buttercups. As we went up the hayfields and over the fallow ground, we saw that this was a fertile island, and suddenly the air was warm and soft. The barley was green and heavy in the ear. The root crops hid the soil. The fields were well barb-wired, but we won through to the pasture-lands at the foot of Dun-I; and there, on impulse, we decided to climb this rock which had so attracted and baffled us from beyond the Treshnish Isles.

We took rather a steep face, but in time we reached the cairn on the top and opened out the west of the island, the green machair land, the sandy bays, the innumerable rocks with the swell breaking on them and throwing its spume high in the air. Here at last was the true Atlantic roar.

. . . The rain seemed to be getting heavier, if that were possible, and we sheltered for a little in the lee of the cairn. In many ways it was a typical West Coast day, with lands and islands vaguely looming and disappearing in the mists. Being properly clad, the rain could not wet us nor the long grasses get over our boots. And this in itself provided a pleasant freedom. The rain, too, kept all folk indoors, so that we saw no human being. We saw the isle itself, and in its coloured fields and soft air, in its sheep grazing here and there and its cattle, we saw also, perhaps more clearly than if the day had been fine, that it was a delectable island. How wisely Columcille had chosen his ground!

Neil M. Gunn: Off in a Boat

THIS ISLAND SET APART

Iona has cast its spell on the sons of men. In early times, it heard the sweet songs of God sung by Saint Columba and his followers. In later days, greater men than we have found there what they sought.

This island set apart, this motherland of many dreams, still yields its secret, but it is only as men seek that they truly find. To reach the heart of Iona is to find something eternal—fresh vision and new courage for every place where love or duty or pain may call us. And he who has so found is ever wishful to return.

* * * * * *

Farewell, then, to Iona. In old days, when they said good-bye in the Gaelic, they said something lovely but so charged with meaning. When husband parted from wife, mother from child, lover from her who was half his sight, they remembered that days might be dreary, friends few, and life hard. But they looked into each other's eyes, and the words always came—"The blessing of God go with you, and the blessing of Columba."

G. E. Troup

RAINN I CHALUM CILLE

Beannachadh I Chalum Cille,
Innis tha beannaichte cheana,
Eilean a tha 'n ìochdar Mhuile,
'S e uile fuidh chis Mhic Cailein;
Ionad naomha a fhuair urram,
Os cionn iomad tìr is fearann,
Ghabhas dìleas ris gach duine
Thig o 'n uile rìoghachd aineal.

'S iomad righ a th' anns an tulaich
'S daoin'-uaisle rìomgach a bharrachd,
'S an ciurp phrìseil bu mhath cumach
Air an leagail sios fo'n talamh;
O 's e deireadh crìch gach duine
Tuiteam 'nan uìr 's 'nam mìn ghaineamh.
Mo dhòchas an Criosd a dh' fhulaing,
Gu'n d'ullaich e sìth d'an anam.

95

Mìle is dà cheud d'a thuille
De bhliadhnachan air dol thairis,
O'n a shuidhich a' cheud duine
Deagh clach-bhunait stéidha' bhalla;
'S iomad dealbh a th' ann a' fuireach
'S leacan nam marbh air dheagh ghearradh,
Clach shnaidhte o'n bhlàr gu mhullach,
'S rinn iad uil' e làidir, fallain.

Fhuair sinn searmoin shoilleir, ullamh,
O'n fhear a bha 'n dé's a chrannaig;
'S chuala mi 'n luchd-éisdeachd uile
Toirt urram do 'n bheul a chan i.
Nis o'n a dh'eug Calum Cille
'S nach bu dù dha féin bhi maireann,
Tha aoibhneas air dùthaich Mhuile
Dùghall a bhi 'n àite Chaluim.

Donnacha Ban (1724-1812)

VERSES ON IONA

A blessing on Icolmkill!
Already blessèd is that isle,
That lies beyond the Ross of Mull
And tribute pays to great Argyll:
That holy place, whose name's renowned
Through many countries east and west,
A welcome has for all who come
Hither to their eternal rest.

Here lie the kings of many a realm,
And gallant gentlemen beside
Who, living, love and valour knew,
But now beneath the dark earth bide;
For 'tis the fate of every man
To fall to fine sand and to moul:
I pray that Christ who died for us
May grant His peace to every soul.

Since the first builder builded here,
Twelve hundred years and more are gone;
'Twas then the basic block was laid
Of this enduring wall of stone.
Full many a form is here preserved
On sculptured tomb, and to the roof
From base the walls are of hewn stone,
Substantial, taut and tempest-proof.

A sermon yesterday I heard
An exposition sound and clear,
And all who heard it honour paid here.
To him whose message drew them
Since Columkill we may not have
(And wishing won't bring back the dead),
Mull and Iona both rejoice
That Dougal* reigns in Colum's stead.

Duncan Ban MacIntyre
(translated by *F. Marian McNeill*)

IONA
(*Upon Landing*)

How sad a welcome! To each voyager
Some ragged child holds up for sale a store
Of wave-worn pebbles, pleading on the shore
Where once came monk and nun with gentle stir,
Blessings to give, news ask, or suit prefer.
Yet is yon neat trim church† a grateful speck

---

* " The Rev. Dougal Campbell, here referred to, was minister of the united parish of Kilfinichen and Kilvickeon, of which Iona then formed a part. It was his duty to preach there every six weeks, and probably the congregation met in the Cathedral, the roof of which was in part still intact. On one of these occasions the poet heard him preach."—Note to Gaelic Songs of Duncan MacIntyre, ed. *George Calder.*

The poem cannot be earlier than 1779, the year in which the Rev. Dougal Campbell was inducted to the charge. This beloved and scholarly minister contributed a description of Iona and its antiquities to the *Old Statistical Account of Scotland* (1795).

† This refers to the Parish Church, not to the Abbey Church. (See editorial note to Wordsworth's Poems.)

97

Of novelty amid the sacred wreck
Strewn far and wide. Think, proud philosopher!
Fallen though she be, this Glory of the West,
Still on her sons the beams of mercy shine,
And hopes, perhaps more heavenly bright than thine,
A grace unsought and unpossest,
A faith more fixed, a rapture more divine
Shall gild their passage to eternal rest!

*William Wordsworth**

FAREWELL TO IONA

Homeward we turn. Isle of Columba's Cell,
Where Christian piety's soul-cheering spark
(Kindled from Heaven between the light and dark
Of time) shone like the morning star, farewell!

William Wordsworth

ISLE OF MY HEART

The beautiful Isles of Greece
Full many a bard has sung;
The isles I love best lie far in the West
Where men speak the Gaelic tongue.
Ithaca, Cyprus, and Rhodes
Are names to the Muses dear;
But sweeter still doth Icolmkill
Fall on a Scotsman's ear.

Alexander Nicolson

COLUMBA'S ISLE

Lone Green isle of the West
   Where the monks, their coracle steering,
Could see no more, o'er the wave's white crest,
   Their own loved home in Erin;
Shrouded often in mist,
   And buried in cloud and rain,
Yet once by the light of a glory kissed,
   Which nothing can dim again!

* Wordsworth visited Iona in 1835, and commemorated his visit
in four indifferent sonnets.

O'er tangled and shell-paved rocks
    The white sea-gulls are flying;
And in the sunny coves brown flocks
    Of wistful seals are lying;
The waves are breaking low:
    Hardly their foam you trace;
All hushed and still, as if they know
    This is a sacred place.

No fitter day than this
    To look on thy mystic beauty
And brood on memories of the bliss
    Of faith and love and duty,
Of the homes of quiet prayer,
    Of the days of patient toil,
Of the love that always and everywhere
    Burned like a holy oil.

Walter C. Smith

THE LORD'S DAY IN IONA

Pure worshipper, who on this holy day
    Wouldst shake thee free from soul-encrusting cares,
And to the great Creator homage pay
    In some high fane most worthy of thy prayers,
Go not where sculptured tower or pictured dome
    Invites the reeking city's jaded throngs,
Some hoar old shrine of Rhineland or of Rome
    Where the dim aisle the languid hymn prolongs;
Here rather follow me, and take thy stand
    By the grey cairn that crowns the lone Dun Ee,
And let thy breezy worship be the grand
    Old bens, and old grey knolls that compass thee,
The sky-blue waters, and the snow-white sand,
    And the quaint isles far-sown upon the sea.

John Stuart Blackie

THE TOURISTS

What brought them here across the briny pool,
A motley train of high and low degree,
Grave seniors, girls whose blue eyes flash with glee,
White-collar'd priests, and boys uncaged from school?
I know not—happy if themselves can tell;
No sights are here to trap the vulgar eye,
No dome whose gilded cross invades the sky,
No palace where wide-sceptred Caesars dwell.
An old grey chapel on an old grey beach,
Grey waste of rocks unpictured by a tree,
And far as hungry vision's range can reach,
The old grey mist upon the old grey sea:
These shows for sense; but the deep truth behind,
They only know who read the mind with mind.

John Stuart Blackie

MOONRISE FROM IONA

Here, where in dim forgotten days
A savage people chanted lays
To long since perished gods, I stand:
The sea breaks in, runs up the sand,
Retreats as with a long-drawn sigh,
Sweeps in again, again leaves dry
The ancient beach, so old and yet
So new that as the strong tides fret
The island barriers in the flow
The ebb-hours of each day can know
A surface change. The day is dead,
The sun is set, and overhead
The white north stars shine keen and bright;
The wind upon the sea is light
And just enough to stir the deep
With phosphorescent gleams and sweep
The spray from salt waves as they rise:
And yonder light—is't from the skies
Some meteor strange, a burning star
Or a lamp hung upon a spar

Of vessel undescried? It gleams
And rises slowly, till it seems
A burning isle, an angel-throne
Re-set on earth, a mountain-cone
Of gold new-risen from sea-caves—
Until at last above the waves,
Set with Atlantic brine, it swims
A silver crescent. Now no hymns
In the wild Runic speech are heard,
No chant, no sacrificial word:
But only mourns the weary sea,
And only the cold wind sings free,
And where the Runic temples stood
The bat flies and the owl doth brood.

William Sharp

THE IONA RAINBOW

(Sung by St. Columba and his monks when putting out to sea)

O Lord of the Heights, whose eye encircles
    The land and the sea, and smiles through the thunder,
Smile on us too, as sail we outward
    To far blue Isles, with tales of the Wonder.

Beyond those waves, strong hearts are longing
    For Heaven's own dream, sweet sounds of the Psalter;
Fair be our breeze, as bear we onward
    Our Christ and our Cross, our song and our altar.

Iona shall grow mid far-off oak-trees,
    The oak-trees shall hear of Love thou awakest;
Aloft in the sky we see thy Rainbow:
    The Druid thou mad'st, the Saint thou remakest.

Beside thy waves our hearts shall praise thee
    For wind and for tide, for share of life's danger;
'Tis well if at eve we make our homeland,
    'Tis well if we sleep the sleep of the stranger.

Kenneth Macleod

101

TO IONA

For their sake who lived and died in thee,
Sang their faith and taught their joy to me,
For their sake I bow the knee,
Iona the blest, *I mo chridh thu*,
Isle of my heart, my grail.

For their sake who hear themselves in thee
Sing of yore thine ancient melodie,
For their sake I bow the knee,
Iona the blest, *I mo chridh thu*,
Isle of my heart, my grail.

For their sake who still shall find in thee
Evermore life's holy artistry,
For their sake I bow the knee,
Iona the blest, *I mo chridh thu*,
Isle of my heart, my grail.

Kenneth Macleod

THOU GRAIL-LIT ISLE

Blue of wave, of hills afar,
Sheen of sand upon the shore,
Night but shrouds them till the dawn
Shall our holden eyes restore.

I-mo-chree, my heart's own isle,
Where monks intoned, now cattle low:
Yet ere hills shall pass away,
Thine altar lights again shall glow.

Where Colum healed the broken wing,
Where he dared the wind-swept kyle,
Where he wondered like a child,
Gleams my holy deathless isle.

I-mo-chree, my heart's own shrine,
Where only lives what seemed to die,
I-mo-chree, my Grail-lit Isle,
Ebb-tide, flow-tide, Christ is nigh.

Kenneth Macleod

IONA

Divine are the mountains,
    The peaks that are trod
By stars to the silence,
    Where only is God.

Divine are the mountains
    Dim seen through the haze;
Divine are your waters,
    The sand in your bays.

The rock-rooted rowan,
    The storm-twisted tree,
The time-scented pasture
    Where murmurs the bee.

The heather-clad moorland,
    The tarn with its rills,
The far purple spaces,
    The sheep on your hills.

Dark Staffa broods yonder,
    There beacons Dun I
To Ulva, and Islay,
    And stormy Tiree.

There flit the rock-pigeons,
    There hovers the gull,
There blaze in the sunset
    The red rocks of Mull.

High crowned with his garland,
    Up-rises Ben More,
Far gleams the tall pillar
    Of lone Skerryvore.

Peace lingers on Earraid,
    The peace of the flocks,
Loud waters of tumult
    Flash white from her rocks.

Or threshed by the tempest
    And swept by the spray,
Or at sleep in the arms
    Of the long summer day.

Art thou, O Iona,
    Of islands most blest,
Where saints have their slumber,
    Where kings have their rest.

What cairn rises yonder?
    What tale does it tell?
Columba bids sadly
    To Erin farewell.

Yet exile of Erin,
    Not ill were thy days,
All thine was this beauty,
    Thy lips give it praise.

Give me, too, in exile,
    The clouds and the breeze,
The stars and the mountains,
    And salt driven seas.

The wishes oft wander,
    The fancy may roam,
But here, O Beloved,
    The heart is at home.

W. Macneile Dixon

IONA

How is it that thou hold'st me thus in thraldom,
O speck of earth begirt by azure sea?
Thou hast no grandeur wild of rugged mountain,
No lonely streams, no wealth of flower or tree.

Yet, mystic isle, what loveliness surrounds thee,
In sea and sky and shimmering silver sand,
The green and purple of translucent waters,
And tinted mists of far-off shadow land:

Or when from Northern seas the hurrying breezes
Uplift the veil; and, to our wondering eyes,
Coolin's dark peaks, Benmore and Jura's mountains,
One bright fair picture stretched before us lies.

And in the glory of day's dying splendour,
When Mull's red rocks with fiery brilliance glow;
Slowly they fade into the waning twilight,
To infinite murmurings of the waters' flow.

Around thy sacred fane, so grey and hoary,
The memories cling—shadows of time long past,
When king and Viking, from the storm of battle,
In thee with hero-saints found peace at last.

Amid the strife, the gloom, of warring ages,
Held by thy sons, the torch of Truth flamed high,
Lighted for anxious men the shadowed valley,
Blessed with new hope the nations far and nigh.

Fled have the years—the kings and kingdoms vanished,
Unchanged art thou: and of a changeless clime,
Dear storied isle, art thou not ever speaking,
Beyond the reach, beyond the realm of time?   *S. D.*

"These verses were written by my mother, a great lover of the
island."—*W. Macneile Dixon.*

IONA

O fair Iona,
Dream-girt Isle,
Guardian of saints and heroes, kings,
Thy ground is holy.
From high Dun-I to thy low green shores,
        white monks have sained thee.

O angel-haunted Isle where Colum trod,
Fair be thy dreams.
O Isle from whence the Light streamed far and wide,
God guard thee from all evil.

Bessie J. B. MacArthur

IONA

With votive offering and earnest prayer,
O Delian island floating on the sea,
I call you shrine of a nation yet to be,
A Scotland of a grander growth and fair;
As once shone Athens bright beyond compare
Out of a rugged land, your people we,
Although down-beaten to our bended knee,
Will yet seek fortune and new danger dare.

If we grow rich in forests and in streams,
In farmlands and the wealth beneath the fields,
Yet still the unconquerable beauty of our land
Will wake our hearts to ever-changing dreams
So strange and fair, we will not drop God's hand,
Or yet forget the far and finer yields.

Archie Lamont

IONA

Upon the white sands foam the waves in splendour,
    Like horses of the Sidhe the billows rise,
Bringing us news and messengers of Faery;
    Harsh with enchanted grief a sea-gull cries.

Luminous gem of peace the isle awaits us,
    Dove-island, heart-enthralling, journey's end;
Small hills allure us, towards the bays englamoured
    By the quick sea, our questing footsteps tend.

Low by the shore, the little church is brooding,
    Grey, peaceful, filled with murmur of the seas;
Here, in the morning, we the Quickening Glory
    Shall meet and worship, lowly on our knees.

Marion Lochhead

106

ROUND THE ISLAND

DUN-I

As I write, here on the hill-slope of Dun-I, the sound of
the furtive wave is as the sighing in a shell. I am alone
between sea and sky, for there is no other on this bouldered
height, nothing visible but a single blue shadow that slowly
sails the hillside. The bleating of lambs and ewes, the
lowing of kine, these come up from the Machar that lies
between the west slopes and the shoreless sea to the west—
these ascend as the very smoke of sound. All around the
island there is a continuous breathing, deeper and more
prolonged in the west, where the open sea is, but audible
everywhere. The seals on Soa are even now putting their
breasts against the running tide; for I see a flashing of fins
here and there in patches at the north end of the Sound, and
already from the ruddy granite shores of the Ross there is a
congregation of seafowl—gannets and guillemots, skuas and
herring-gulls, the long-necked northern diver, the tern, the
cormorant. In the sunblaze, the waters of the Sound dance
their blue bodies and swirl their flashing white hair o' foam;
and, as I look, they seem to me like children of the wind and
the sunshine, leaping and running in these flowing pastures,
with a laughter as sweet against the ears as the voices of
children at play.

The joy of life vibrates everywhere.

. . . I stop, and look seaward from this hill-slope of
Dun-I. Yes, even in this Isle of Joy, as it seems in this
dazzle of golden light and splashing wave, there is the like
mortal gloom and immortal mystery which moved the minds
of the old seers and bards. Yonder, where that thin spray
quivers against the thyme-set cliff, is the Spouting Cave,

107

where to this day the Mar-Tarbh, dread creature of the sea, swims at the full of the tide. Beyond, out of sight behind these scraggy steeps, is Port-na-Churaich, where, a thousand years ago, Columba landed in his coracle. Here, eastward, is the landing-place for the dead of old, brought hence out of Christendom for sacred burial in the Isle of the Saints. All the story of the Gael is here. Iona is the microcosm of the Gaelic world.*

Fiona Macleod: Iona

TOBAR NA H-AOIS
THE POOL OF HEALING

On the northern brow of Dun-I, not a stone's throw from where I lie, half-hidden beneath an overhanging rock, is the Pool of Healing. To this small, black-brown tarn, pilgrims of every generation, for hundreds of years, have come. Solitary, these; not only because the pilgrim to the Fount of Eternal Youth must fare hither alone, and at dawn, so as to touch the healing water the moment the first sunray quickens it—but solitary, also, because those who go in quest of this Fount of Youth are the dreamers of the Children of Dream, and these are not many, and few come now to this lonely place. Yet, an Isle of Dream Iona is indeed. Here the last sun-worshippers bowed before the rising of God; here Columba and his hymning priests laboured and brooded; and here Oran or his kin dreamed beneath the monkish cowl that pagan dream of his. Here, too, the eyes of Fionn and Oisín, and of many another of the heroic men and women of the Fiànna, may have lingered; here the Pict and the Celt bowed beneath the yoke of the Norse pirate, who, too, left his dreams, or rather his strangely beautiful soul-rainbows, as a heritage to the stricken; here, for century after century, the Gael has lived, suffered, joyed, dreamed his impossible beautiful dream; as here, now, he still lives, still suffers patiently, still dreams, and through all and over all broods upon the incalculable mysteries. He is an elemental, among the elemental forces. He knows the

* This is the revised form of a letter written from Iona to George Meredith, and used as a dedication to the volume, *The Sin-Eater*.

108

voices of wind and sea; and it is because the Fount of Youth upon Dun-I of Iona is not the only well-spring of peace that the Gael can front destiny as he does and can endure. Who knows where its tributaries are? They may be in your heart, or in mine, and in a myriad others.

Fiona Macleod: Iona

DUN MANANAIN

(From Tobar na h-Aois, Well of the Age, known also as the Fountain of Youth—a triangular pool of water beside a small crag on the northern brow of Dùn-I) I turned, and walked idly northward, down the rough side of Dun Bhuirg . . . to a thyme-covered mound that had for me a most singular fascination.

It is a place to this day called Dun Mananain. Here, a friend who told me many things, a Gaelic farmer, named Macarthur, had related once a fantastic legend about a god of the sea. Manaun was his name, and he lived in the times when Iona was part of the kingdom of the Suderöer. Whenever he willed he was like the sea, and that is not wonderful, for he was born of the sea. Thus his body was made of a green wave. His hair was of wrack and tangle, glistening with spray; his robe was of windy foam; his feet of white sand. That is, when he was with his own, or when he willed; otherwise, he was as men are. He loved a woman of the south so beautiful that she was named Dèarsadh-na-Ghréine (Sunshine). He captured her and brought her to Iona in September, when it is the month of peace. For one month she was happy; when the wet gales from the west set in, she pined for her own land, yet in the dream-days of November she smiled so often that Manaun hoped; but when winter was come, her lover saw that she could not live. So he changed her into a seal. " You shall be a sleeping woman by day," he said, " and sleep in my dun here on Iona, and by night, when the dews fall, you shall be a seal, and shall hear me calling to you from a wave, and shall come out and meet me."

They have mortal offspring also, it is said.

... That summer I had been thrilled to the inmost life
by coming suddenly, by moonlight, on a seal moving across
the last sand-dune between this place and the bay called
Port Ban. A strange voice, too, I heard upon the sea. True,
I saw no white arms upthrown, as the seal plunged into the
long wave that swept the shore; and it was a grey skua that
wailed above me, winging inland; yet had I not had a
vision of the miracle?

But alas! that evening there was not even a barking
seal. Some sheep fed upon the green slope of Manaun's
mound.

Fiona Macleod: Iona

TRAIGH BHAN NAM MANACH
(*White Strand of the Monks*)

The sweet-sounding plash of the light rippling billows,
    As they beat on the sand where the white pebbles lie,
And their shuddering roar when with wheeling commotion
    They lift their white crests in grim face of the sky.

ST. ORAN'S CHAPEL AND QUEEN MARGARET

The little roofless chapel, down in the corner to the left,
and dedicated to St. Oran, the oldest of the ruins, is
probably eleventh century. That Saxon and pious queen,
Margaret, wife of Malcolm Canmore, is believed to have had
it built as one of her efforts to civilise the savages of her
adopted country. She stuck hard to her thankless task,
yet with such success that good Scottish historians to this
day bless her name. And as far as these Highland parts are
concerned, her reforms slowly but surely spread until their
feudalistic groundwork blossomed in the flame-bright
flower of the Clearances. She was a pious statesman, whose
sad and onerous duty, to herself and to God, was to spread
the light in that heathen darkness where, long centuries
before her redeeming advent, a benighted successor to
Columcille was writing: "At another time, while the
blessed man was living in the Iouan Island (Iona), one day
his holy face lighted up with a certain wondrous and

110

joyous cheerfulness, and, lifting up his eyes to heaven, filled with incomparable joy, he was intensely gladdened." They believed in those far days that " when the heart is glad the face blooms." Such simple and dogged cheerfulness must be a sad trial to any true reformer. But she did her best.

Neil M. Gunn: Off in a Boat

THE ABBEY CHURCH

The interior had more than the bareness of the usual Scottish country church, for the walls themselves were bare stones; yet from these stones came a real effect of light, wonderfully heightened by what appeared on that dull day to be a long low altar of greenish-white glowing stone. Midway on this altar stood a narrow brass vase of flowers— white irises and blue and pink delphiniums—so perfectly arranged that they were a burgeoning of light and colour, an aspiration, a loveliness. The Crew could hardly take her eyes off them, as we stood in the nave at some little distance. And in truth I must confess I have rarely encountered so direct a manifestation of ineffable harmony.

But the harmony of the whole interior was destroyed by two massive recumbent effigies in white marble of a Duke and Duchess of Argyll occupying almost all the southern transept. One hesitates to write one's full thought about it. At the best, how sad and hopeless this heavy effort at immortality compared with the spirit that fed the birds or even the nameless hands that had arranged the flowers. Perhaps, but for these two in life, the modern church or cathedral would not have been there. We did not enquire.

Outside, again, we stood before the great Cross of Iona, dedicated to St. Martin of Tours, the friend of St. Ninian. It has the easy, incomparable grace of the true Celtic Cross, strong, sure in workmanship, and at rest. You could feel the harmony behind the chisel that hewed it.

Neil M. Gunn: Off in a Boat

111

EVENING WORSHIP IN THE ABBEY IN TIME OF WAR

Blow in, salt wind, through chinks,
Out of the night,
And toss the candle-light!

Contorted flames burn up and flicker down,
The twisted shadows flit;
The Abbey stands beleaguered by the storm,
The gale assaulting it.
Without, the moonstruck madness of the wind;
Within, strange peace,
Sea-deep, rock-rooted, old, immutable.
Calm does not cease
Within these walls. Here time stands still and waits;
And no clock ticks
The hours for Satan's screaming orators
To loose their tricks
Against the world poised on a pinnacle,
Falling askew
To the abyss. Yet may God's steady hand
Hold balance true.

Salt wind, blow in, through chinks,
Out of the night;
The candle-flame burns bright.

Agnes A. C. Blackie

COLUMBA'S TOMB

Near to the west end of the church in a little cell lies
Columbus's tomb, but without inscription. This gave me
occasion to cite the distich, asserting that Columbus was
buried in Ireland, at which the natives of Iona seemed very
much displeased, and affirmed that the Irish who said so
were impudent liars; that Columbus was once buried in
this place, and that none ever came from Ireland, since to
carry away his corpse, which, had they attempted, would
have proved equally vain and presumptuous.

Martin Martin: A Description of the Western
Islands of Scotland (circa 1695)

THE BLACK STONES OF IONA

A little further to the west (of *Dun na Manach,* or
Monk's Fort) lie the Black Stones, which are so called, not
from their colour, for that is grey, but from the effects that
tradition say ensued upon perjury, if any one became guilty
on it after swearing on these stones in the usual manner; for
an oath made on them was decisive in all controversies.

Macdonald, King of the Isles, delivered the rights of
their lands to his vassals in the isles and continent, with
uplifted hands and bended knees, on the black stones; and
in this posture, before many witnesses, he solemnly swore
that he would never recall those rights which he then granted;
and this was instead of his Great Seal. Hence it is that when
one was certain of what he affirmed, he said positively, I
have freedom to swear this matter upon the Black Stones.*

Martin Martin: A Description of the Western
Islands of Scotland (circa 1695)

CLACH BRATH

Until the Synod of Argyll destroyed them, three globes
of white marble lay in hollows on a stone slab beside
St. Oran's, and a visitor to the island had to turn the stones
thrice sunwise—deisul (thus Druidically performing the
rites of sun worship on the way to the worship of God).
The slab (Clach Brath) is still there, with the hollows upon
it, and until quite recent times the natives used to turn
three ordinary stone balls in the hollows three times deisul,
for luck, every time they passed. But these later stones
have gone too.

Neil M. Gunn: Off in a Boat

IN THE NUNNERY GARDEN†

Within this cloistered fabric, old and grey,
Roofless, turf-floored, with arches incomplete,
Spring from the broken walls and crevices
Colour and fragrance sweet.

* The last of these stones disappeared a century or more ago.

† The ruined nunnery has been converted into a beautiful garden
in memory of Mrs. K. J. Spencer, by her children.

Plumes of valerian, crimson, pink and white,
Spires of blue lupin, blue as Chalbha seas,
Great scarlet poppy-heads, and columbine,
 And gentle-eyed heartsease.

Rosemary, lavender, the sharp sweetbrier,
Clusters of wallflower, tawny-red and gold,
Shy little rock-plants in their granite beds
 Groping to find a hold.

So may your House of Life, as years increase,
Harbour bright graces tho' the walls decay:
Courage and faith, tenacious as these flowers
 And beautiful as they.

Helen B. Cruickshank

THE COVE OF THE CORACLE

There are many pretty variegated stones on the shore below the dock; they ripen to a green colour, and are then proper for carving. The natives say these stones are fortunate, but only for some particular thing, which the person thinks fit to name, in exclusion of everything else.

Martin Martin: A Description of the Western
Isles of Scotland (circa 1695)

The pebbly beach of green quartz, hornblende, and red felspar on which Columba landed over thirteen hundred years ago is still there, the beautiful sea-bugloss expanding its glistening petals from pink to blue, as when he moved from place to place conversing with his brethren; and, perhaps, the root and seeds of the sea-holly and marsh trefoil that arrested the eye of the pilgrim who came for sanctuary and purification, or to seek a blessing on a perilous venture.

Hugh MacDiarmid: The Islands of Scotland
(*B. T. Batsford, Ltd.*)

114

Our first expedition was to the Port 'a Churaich (Port of the Coracle) at the southern end of the island, where, according to strong local tradition, St. Columba first landed. It is a pleasant scrambling walk (in Iona there are few paths and one goes wherever one pleases). Cuckoos were calling loudly among the rocks where small brown birds nested, and larks were singing rapturously. A wonderful variety of flowers were opening, and every day that we spent in the island the gay company increased. Irises thronged the little glens and climbed the steep slopes, and daily they unfurled more of their gay yellow flags from the fat green sheaths. Almost treeless as the island is, primroses and bluebells flourished in the more sheltered angles of the rocks. The vernal squill, a flower like a very dainty scilla that was new to us, grew on the driest, most exposed knolls. The turf was variegated with the tiny faces of milkwort, crowsfoot, potentilla, eye-bright, speedwell, and a wee everlasting flower in pink and white. Mauve wild orchises were everywhere, stonecrop and a pretty white sedum fringed the rocks. Marsh-marigold, butterwort, bog-bean and the pinkish rosettes of the sundew made the boggy patches gay. Buttercups and daisies turned the pasture-land into sheets of silver and gold. The floor of the bay itself was almost as full of varied colour as the flowers, for pebbles more brightly coloured than any we had ever seen caught the sunlight through the clear, green water.

I. F. Grant: The Lordship of the Isles

PORT NA CHURAICH

" *Ere the world shall come to an end, Iona shall be as it was.*"

Changeless, beneath the changing skies,
It lies,
That crescent shore—
Bordered for evermore
With glowing gems, as fair
As though the lovely thoughts of Colum Cill', long
    hovering there,
Had slowly crystallised in jewels rare.

Swift glides the coracle to land:
The strand
Is flaming bright,
With monkish figures white:
And in the air,
A chanted cadence, sweet and strange,
As though a change
Mysterious, fair,
Had fallen on the island unaware.

And now it fades—yet still the crescent gleams,
And dreams
Predestinate disturb the air:
Prophetic words unsheath anew their wings—
The island stirs—and everywhere
Is rumour of incalculable things.

Bessie J. B. MacArthur

THE MACHAIR

Last night, about the hour of the sun's going, I lay upon the heights near the cave, overlooking the Machar— the sandy, rock-frontiered plain of duneland on the west side of Iona, exposed to the Atlantic. There was neither bird nor beast, no living thing to see, save one solitary human creature. The man toiled at kelp-burning. I watched the smoke till it merged into the sea-mist that came creeping swiftly out of the north, and down from Dun-I eastward. At last nothing was visible. The mist shrouded everything. I could hear the dull, rhythmic beat of the waves. That was all. No sound, nothing visible.

It was, or seemed, a long while before a rapid thud-thud trampled the heavy air. Then I heard the rush, the stamping and neighing, of some young mares, pasturing there, as they raced to and fro, bewildered or perchance in play. A glimpse I caught of three, with flying manes and tails; the others were blurred shadows only. A swirl, and the mist disclosed them; a swirl, and the mist enfolded them again. Then, silence once more.

Abruptly, though not for a long time thereafter, the mist rose and drifted seaward.

All was as before. The kelp-burner still stood, straking the mouldering seaweed. Above him a column ascended, bluely spiral, dusked with shadow.

The kelp-burner; who was he but the Gael of the Isles? Who but the Gael in his old-world sorrow? The mist falls and the mist rises. He is there all the same, behind it, part of it; and the column of smoke is the incense out of his longing heart that desires Heaven and Earth, and is dowered only with poverty and pain, hunger and weariness, a little isle of the seas, a great hope, and the love of love.

Fiona Macleod: The Isle of Dreams

THE SEA-ROCKET

Lovely upon the lonely shore
I came upon a solitary flower.
Rooted in sand she was, while every hour
The sea-wind whistled o'er
Her comfortable strength.
On all the length
Of the long beach the only flower was she.
Sturdy and strong, the neighbour of the sea.

Delicate her petal as an angel's gown,
Her stout leaf bright and thick,
Her seed-pod like the mitre on a bishop's crown,
Her lonely bishopric
Amid the shifting sands forever cast.
Tread lightly, stranger! This way God has passed.

Isobel Wylie Hutchison

117

REILIG ODHRAIN

AN ANCIENT PROPHECY
As was natural for soil so sacred, Iona became a great place of sepulchre; but the desire of so many kings, chiefs and prelates to be buried there may have been increased by the ancient prophecy:—

Seachd bliadhna roimh 'n bhràth,
Thig muir thar Eirinn ré aon tràth,
'S thar Ile ghuirm ghlais,
Ach snàmhaidh I Choluim chléirich.

Seven years before the Judgment
The sea shall sweep over Erin at one tide,
And over blue-green Isla,
But the Island of Columba
Shall swim above the flood.

IONA BOAT SONG
It was to the inlet known as Martyrs' Bay (the scene of the first recorded slaughter of the monks by the Danes in 806), just south of the village, that the galleys and barges of old brought the distinguished dead of many centuries. Opposite the bay is a low green mound called Eala, and here the bodies were laid for a space, while the mourners gathered round to " pour their wailing o'er the dead." Sraid na Maraibh (the Street of the Dead), which leads from the bay to Reilig Odhrain, marks the route of the funeral trains of old.
A galley approaches the shore.

118

Iomair o, 'illean mhara,
Iomair o.
Isle of deeps, where death ne'er weepeth,
Sails to thee a king who sleepeth,
With thy saints the Tryst he keepeth,
Iomair o, 'illean mhara,
Iomair o.

Kenneth Macleod

REILIG ODHRAIN

" Within this Isle of Kilmkill there is ane Sanctuary also, or Kirkzaird, called in Erishe (Erse) Releag Oran. In it are three tombs of staine formit like little chapels, with ane braide grey quin stane in the gairle of ilk ane of the tombes. In the staine of ane is written—Tumulus Regum Scotiae, that is, the Tomb of the Scottes Kings—within this there lay 48 crowned Scottes Kings. The tomb on the south side has this inscription—Tumulus Regum Hiberniae, that is, the Tomb of the Ireland Kings; there were four Ireland Kings in it. Upon the north side of our Scottes tomb the inscription bears—Tumulus Regum Norwegiae, the Tomb of the Kings of Norroway. Within this sanctuary lye also the maist part of the Lords of the Isles, with their lynage; twa Clan Leans, with their lynage; McKinnon and McQuarrie, with their lynage, with sundrie uther inhabitants of the haille isles.

Donald Monro (*Dean of the Isles*): Description
of the Western Isles of Scotland (1549)

Of these celebrated tombs we could discover nothing more than certain slight remains, that were built in a ridged form, and arched within: but the inscriptions were lost.

Pennant: Voyage to the Hebrides (1772)

The ruins of I, by the generous care and attention of the family of Argyll, are kept, perhaps, in better preservation than most ruins of the kind in Scotland.

The Old Statistical Account of Scotland (1798)

119

The Iona Club in 1833, by permission of the President, his Grace the Duke of Argyll, made some searches in this ancient cemetery, for such tombstones as might have been concealed by the accumulation of rubbish; and the result of their operations was, that a considerable number of finely-carved tombstones were brought to view, which none of the inhabitants had ever before seen. These were placed upon the surface of the cemetery.

The New Statistical Account (1845)

Forty-eight Scottish kings buried in this tumbled graveyard—*before* the Norman conquest of England in 1066. And to-day should a man be bold enough to refer to the Scottish nation, he is looked upon as a bit of a crank, and his brothers smile for him, with diffident humour, in apology. St. Margaret of blessed memory worked better than she knew, and certainly her husband, Malcolm Canmore, broke the Iona tradition by being buried properly in Dunfermline.

As late as 1594, the Dean of the Isles describes three tombs, " formit like little Chapels "; *Tumulus Regum Scotiae, Tumulus Regum Hiberniae,* and *Tumulus Regum Norwegiae.* In the first " there lay fortey-eight crowned Scotts Kings." In the others, Irish and Norwegian Kings. " Within this sanctuary also lye maist pairt of the Lords of the Isles, with their lynage, twa clan Leans, with their lynage, with sundrie uthers, inhabitants of the haill isles."

There is little evidence of all this temporal glory to be seen now, though the two ridges—the Ridge of the Kings and the Ridge of the Chiefs—are clear enough. . . . Altogether it is a small unimpressive place—to the mind looking for physical wonders.

But to a mind otherwise concerned limitless are the perspectives that open out. There can be little doubt, for example, but that Druidism and Christianity meet here, as the story of Oran so searchingly illustrates.

Neil M. Gunn: Off in a Boat

THE SEPULCHRE OF KINGS
Scene: Outside Macbeth's Castle

ROSS: Here comes the good Macduff.
How goes the world, sir, now?

MACDUFF: Why, see you not?

ROSS: Is't known who did this more than bloody deed?

MACDUFF: Those that Macbeth hath slain.

ROSS: Alas the day!
What good could they pretend?

MACDUFF: They were suborn'd:
Malcolm and Donalbain, the king's two sons,
Are stol'n away and fled, which puts upon them
Suspicion of the deed.

ROSS: 'Gainst nature still:
Thriftless ambition, that will ravin up
Thine own life's means! Then 'tis most like
The sovereignty will fall upon Macbeth.

MACDUFF: He is already named, and gone to Scone
To be invested.

ROSS: Where is Duncan's body?

MACDUFF: Carried to Colme-kill,
The sacred storehouse of his predecessors
And guardian of their bones.

*   *   *   *   *   *   *

MACBETH: Better be with the dead
Whom we, to gain our peace, have sent to peace,
Than on the torture of the mind to lie
In restless ecstasy. Duncan is in his grave;
After life's fitful fever he sleeps well;
Treason has done his worst; not steel, nor
poison,
Malice domestic, foreign levy, nothing
Can touch him further!

Shakespeare: Macbeth, Act II, Sc. 4; Act III, Sc. 2

THE GHOSTS WALK

Unbounded is thy range, with varied stile
  Thy muse may, like those feath'ry tribes which spring
From their rude rocks, extend her skirting wing
  Round the moist maze of each cold Hebrid isle.

Thither, where beneath the show'ry west
 The mighty kings of three fair realms are laid;
Once foes, perhaps, together now they rest.
 No slaves revere them, and no wars invade:
Yet frequent now, at midnight's solemn hour,
 The rifted mounds their yawning cells unfold,
And forth the monarchs stalk with sov'reign power
 In pageant robes, and wreathed like sheening gold,
And on their twilight tombs aerial council hold.

William Collins: (1721-1759) Ode on the
Popular Superstitions of the Highlands

THE LORD OF THE ISLES

And this is the manner in which a Lord of the Isles
would die: Monks and priests being over him, and he having
received the Body of Christ, and the Holy Oil having been
put upon him, his fair body was brought to Iona of Columcille. And the abbot and the monks and the vicars came
forth to meet him, as it was the custom to meet the body of
the King of the Isles; and his service and waking were
honourably performed during eight days and eight nights;
after which, his full noble body was laid in the same grave
with his fathers, in the Reilig of Oran.

Kenneth Macleod: The Road to the Isles

ANGUS OG
ANGUS MACDONALD OF ISLAY AND KINTYRE

*(Angus Og, or Young Angus, was a close friend of
Robert Bruce, with whom he fought at Bannockburn. He was
a renowned warrior, and is the hero of Sir Walter Scott's
" Lord of the Isles," though his name (says Scott in a note)
was changed to Ronald for the sake of euphony.)*

The heir of mighty Somerled,
Ronald from many a hero sprung,
The fair, the valiant and the young
Lord of the Isles, whose lofty name
A thousand bards have given to fame,
The mate of monarchs, and allied
On equal terms with England's pride.

Sir Walter Scott: Lord of the Isles

O hone a rie!* O hone a rie!
  The pride of Albin's line is o'er,
And fall'n Glenartney's stateliest tree:
  We ne'er shall see Lord Ronald more!
    Scott: Glenfinlas, or Lord Ronald's Coronach

EASPUIG AOIDH CAMO-CHASACH
(BISHOP HUGH OF THE CROOKED LEGS)
" The Abbot comes!" they cry at once,
" The holy man whose favoured glance
  Hath sainted visions known;
Angels have met him on the way
Beside the blessed Martyrs' Bay
  And to Columba's Stone.
His monks have heard their hymnings high
Sound from the summit of Dun-Y
  To cheer his penance lone."
    Scott: The Lord of the Isles

MACLEAN OF COLL†
(*Late Fifteenth Century*)
And in his hand a sheathèd sword
Such as few arms could wield;
But when he bound him to the task,
Well could it cleave the strongest casque
And rend the surest shield.
    Scott: The Lord of the Isles

A DISTINGUISHED PHYSICIAN
DR. JOHN BETON
A succession of an order of literati, named Ollamh
(learned men) existed in Mull from time immemorial until
the middle of the last (eighteenth) century. . . . The last
of the order was the famous old Dr. John Beton, physican

* Alas for the prince (or chief)!

† Dr. Johnson and Boswell were entertained in the island of Coll
by the chief of their day, and speak affectionately of " young Coll,"
who was drowned soon after their visit.

123

to James VII and II. His memory is preserved in Iona by the tombstone, erected by a relation, with the following inscription:—

HIC . JACET . IONNES . BETONUS . MACLENORUM . FAMILIAE . MEDIC⁸ QUI . MORTUS . EST . 19 . NOWEMBRIS . ANNO . DOMINI . 1657 . ET . ETATIS . SVE . 63 . DONALDUS . BETONUS . ME . FECIT . 1674 . ECCE . CADIT . IACULO . VICTRICI . MORTIS . INIQUI . QUI . TOTIES . ALIOS . SOLVERAT . IPSE . MALIS . SOLI . DEO . GLORIA.

(Here lies John Beton, physician to the family of the Macleans, who died 19 *January,* 1657, *aged* 63. *Donald Beton made me* 1674. *Behold, he who saved so many others from ills, himself falls by the conquering dart of wicked Death. Glory to God alone.)*

H. D. Graham: Antiquities of Iona

WESTWARD

(FOR MARJORY KENNEDY-FRASER)

Mrs. Kennedy-Fraser, who with Kenneth Macleod collected and edited the Songs of the Hebrides, died in Edinburgh in 1930. Her ashes were carried to Iona and interred in Reilig Odhrain in 1932.

Far have I gone and come by stream and down,
    O'er many a valley wandered, many a hill,
And many a street in my remembered town
    Trod with goodwill.

But now about me wild the breakers roar,
    And now I seek the storm and in the west
Take with the shining sea-wrack on the shore
    My rest.

Isobel Wylie Hutchison

LOST LADYE?

O siller, siller shone the mune
An' quaiet swang the door,
An' eerie skraighed the flaughtered gulls
As she gaed by the shore.

124

O saft tae her the meadow girse,
But set wi' rock the hill,
An' scored wi' bluid her ladye feet
Or she cam' the place intill.

The sheen o' steel was in her hand,
The sheen o' stars in her een,
An' she wad open the fairy hill
An' she wad let oot the queen.

*   *   *   *   *   *   *

There cam' a shepherd owre the hill
When day began tae daw;
And is this noo a seggit ewe
Or flourish frae the schaw?

It wasna lamb nor seggit ewe
Nor flourish frae the schaw,
It was the ladye bright an' still,
But she had won awa'.

The peace an' loveliness upon
Her broo said, ' *Lat abee,*
Here fand I that I sairly socht,
Ye needna peety me.'

Helen B. Cruickshank

This poem commemorates the tragedy of a lady, a visitor to Iona, who fell a victim to " the lure of the fairy hill." One moonlight night she slipped out of the cottage where she was staying, unclad, with a knife in her hand (with which to open the hill), and in the early morning her body was found beside the *Sithean Mor* (great fairy mound) near the Machair. She was buried in Reilig Odhrain. The incident occurred within the present century.

THE *GUY MANNERING*

Among the modern gravestones of Reilig Odhrain is a monument erected by the United States to sixteen persons drowned in the wreck of the American ship *Guy Mannering* on the west coast of the island, on the last day of 1865.

E. C. Trenholme: The Story of Iona

EPILOGUE

MEN ON ISLANDS

Can it be that never more
Men will grow on Islands?
Ithaka and Eriskay,
Iceland and Tahati!
Must the engines he has forged
Raven so for spaces
That the Islands dwindle down,
Dwindle down!
Pots that shelve the tap-roots' growth?
Must it be that never more
Men will flower on Islands?
Crete and Corsica, Mitylene,
Aran and Iona!

Padraic Colum

A POET'S VIEW

The more intimately one gets to know these islands [of
Scotland], the more one discerns the utter falsity of the
Celtic Twilight school and finds all its high-falutin
descriptions intolerable, remembering what George

126

Macdonald says: " For the very essence of poetry is truth, and as soon as a word's not true, it's not poetry, though it may wear the cast clothes of it "; and one comes greatly to prefer the laconic style of Dean Monro, who simply says Mull is " ane grate rough isle " and describes one of its minor satellites, with perfect accuracy, as " ane rockie knobb."

It must not be too readily assumed, however, that even the best known and most frequently visited of the Scottish islands are really knowable to people without certain special qualifications at all. [He deplores in particular the general ignorance of both Gaelic and the Norn of Orkney and Shetland] . . . Of course in saying this I must not be taken as sharing the notion that the Hebrides are an arcane affair accessible only to the natives by whom they are run like lamaseries in Thibet for the cultivation of rare states of mind, peculiar psychological powers, and other high mysteries. . . . I have no regard of any sort for the mahatmas of this cult.

. . . Reflecting on these islands—on, say, Barra or Iona—on the attainments of past ages, one can hardly but be disposed to conclude that it is we who are the savages, in gross and in detail, in the unobtrusive as well as in the more shocking ways of savagery. It must seem that the world has lost something it once possessed, that Europe at any rate has been living for the past fifteen hundred years or a little more under a grave misapprehension as to the nature of things, perhaps deliberately brought about by those who ought to have known better. If so, it is well that some should bring back to us what was lost. There is an extensive and learned literature which searches the externals of the subject, beginning from the outside; there are also authors who write with an inward knowledge—but these are few and far between. How are we to test the authenticity of what they proffer? . . . My knowledge makes me slow to concede the claims of many . . . who seem to any considerable public to write concerning these matters with silver tongues of beauty and wisdom, though what they purport to give are, indeed, the streams for which I thirst—

127

judgment that proceeds by vision, government that springs from insight, art in which the artist is anonymous, temples whose priests do not mouth the fragments of uncomprehended formulas but say what they have seen and heard and known in the spirit. Is this a vision of the past or the future or of both? We shall see.

. . . There is a very generally entertained idea that to live on an island is to be " out of things "—an assumption that great significance for humanity is more likely to attach itself to big centres of population—to London rather than Eriskay, say. I see no reason for assuming anything of the sort. . . . " It is a remarkable fact," writes Th. A. Fischer, author of *The Scots in Germany*, " that in the history of the development of the human mind the great spiritual movements did not always proceed from the most famous and the most powerful nations or cities, the so-called centres of intelligence, but, similar to the mighty rivers of the world, had their sources in localities small, hidden and unknown." . . . No matter how many millions may be congregated into great cities like London and New York, there is nothing inherently impossible or even improbable in Dr. Johnson's remark that " perhaps, in the revolutions of the world, Iona may be some time again the instructress of the Western regions," a statement echoing St. Columba's own prediction in the verse which, being translated, reads: " Iona of my heart, Iona of my love! Where now is the chanting of monks, there will be lowing of cattle. But before the world is ended, Iona will be as it was."

Hugh MacDiarmid: The Islands of Scotland

THE FUTURE

" Columba was a prophet, and prophets care little for that phantasy called Time."—*The Coracle.*

In Iona of my heart, Iona of my love,
Instead of monks' voices shall be lowing of cattle;
But ere the world come to an end,
Iona shall be as it was.